When the baseball season opened in Jersey City on the Passaic River, it was always a big deal. Excitement crackled like fireworks in Roosevelt Stadium.

Schools were shut down so the children could see the game. City workers got the day off. Today saw a sellout crowd of 25,000 under brilliant spring sunshine. The hometown Jersey City Giants were playing the Montreal Royals.

But this day—April 18, 1946—was even more electric than usual. World War II had just ended, and minor league baseball was being played again. All eyes today would be on a rookie player with the Montreal Royals. Some of the fans were thrilled to see him there, and others hated the very sight of him. But everyone sensed that history was being made today.

A Background Note about
Jackie Robinson: An American Hero

When Jackie Robinson was born in Georgia in 1919, American society was separate and unequal. In the South, a cruel system of segregation denied black Americans the rights that white Americans took for granted. Blacks were barred from attending the same schools as whites. Nor could they go to the same parks, libraries, hospitals, restaurants, or auditoriums. On trains and buses, they were forced to sit apart from whites, usually in back. The few places that catered to blacks were always inferior. Many blacks were forcibly prevented from voting. Although things were a little better in the North, blacks were still denied equal opportunities for advancement. Not surprisingly, an unwritten policy also barred blacks from participating in the national pastime, major league baseball. But by the end of World War II, things had begun to change. Returning black veterans argued that if they were good enough to fight for their country, they deserved equal rights. They demanded an end to segregation. Civil rights leaders stepped up their pressure on elected officials. And baseball's color barrier was about to be broken by one courageous individual: Jack Roosevelt Robinson.

JACKIE ROBINSON

An American Hero

Anne Schraff

 THE TOWNSEND LIBRARY

JACKIE ROBINSON:
An American Hero

TP THE TOWNSEND LIBRARY

For more titles in the Townsend Library,
visit our website: www.townsendpress.com

Copyright © 2008 by Townsend Press
Printed in the United States of America

0 9 8 7 6 5 4 3 2

Illustrations © 2008 by Hal Taylor

Townsend Press, Inc.
439 Kelley Drive
West Berlin, NJ 08091
cs@townsendpress.com

ISBN-13: 978-1-59194-102-6
ISBN-10: 1-59194-102-4

Library of Congress Control Number:
2007943678

Contents

CHAPTER 1
The First Victory 1

CHAPTER 2
A Mother's Courage 7

CHAPTER 3
A Fatherless Boy 19

CHAPTER 4
The Four-Sport Star 28

CHAPTER 5
The Soldier and the Nurse 45

CHAPTER 6
The Brave Experiment 63

CHAPTER 7
Grace Under Pressure 80

CHAPTER 8
Champions at Sundown 93

CHAPTER 9
Fighting for Equality 107

CHAPTER 10
Jackie Robinson Steals Home 120

Chapter 1

The First Victory

When the baseball season opened in Jersey City on the Passaic River, it was always a big deal. Excitement crackled like fireworks in Roosevelt Stadium. Schools were shut down so the children could see the game. City workers got the day off. Today saw a sellout crowd of 25,000 under brilliant spring sunshine. The hometown Jersey City Giants were playing the Montreal Royals.

But this day—April 18, 1946—was even more electric than usual. World War II had just ended, and minor league baseball was being played again. All eyes today would be on a rookie player with the Montreal Royals. Some of the fans were thrilled to see him there, and some hated the very sight of him. But everyone sensed that history was being made today.

Twenty-eight-year-old Jackie Robinson, a tall, handsome man with black skin, was breaking the color barrier of baseball. He would be the first black man in the 20th century to play organized baseball. Up until now, no black athlete could play, no matter how good he was at the game.

There was a big difference in the baseball crowd that day. The fans were not just from Jersey City. People had come from New York, Philadelphia, Boston, Baltimore and places even farther away. Some white fans had come to see what would happen when a black man took the field for the first time. The many black fans had come to share in what was a proud moment.

The press box was packed, and there were many photographers around the field. When Robinson and his teammates marched to deep center field for the raising of the Stars and Stripes and the singing of "The Star-Spangled Banner," black fans sang with more spirit than they had ever sung with before. It was as if the voices rose through their bodies in a great wave.

Jackie Robinson described his feelings at that moment with these words. He said he stood there watching the flag rippling in the sunshine "with a lump in my throat and my heart beating rapidly, my stomach feeling as if it were full of feverish fireflies with claws on their feet."

Mayor Frank Hague tossed out the first ball. On wobbly legs, Robinson walked to the batter's box. Robinson was pigeon-toed, and that made his step even shakier. A hundred thoughts rushed through his mind.

What would the crowd do when they saw this black man playing the national pastime of baseball? Would there be violence? Would there be ugly scenes? The idea of blacks entering major league baseball had been violently opposed by many whites.

Jackie Robinson's wife, Rachel, was there in the stands. Would she be safe? Would some unstable racist take out his frustration on her? Rachel Robinson did not remain seated. She paced through the aisles nervously.

Robinson stood at home plate, forcing himself to focus on the game and not look out at the fans. He feared that the blacks would cheer him and the whites would yell insults or remain coldly silent, freezing him out. The crowd applauded politely, but not warmly.

Robinson's knees shook, and the palms of his hands were so wet with perspiration that he could hardly hold the bat. He did not swing at the first pitches, but then he hit a bouncing ball to the shortstop, who easily threw him out. No matter: the ice had been broken. As Robinson hurried back to the dugout, light applause greeted him. He had made his first appearance, got his bat on the ball, and the world, at least, had not ended.

The first inning was scoreless. Robinson did not bat again until the third inning. With two runners on base, Robinson knew he had to calm down and focus. The Jersey City pitcher was determined not to be the first pitcher to give up a hit to Robinson. But Jackie was more determined.

On the very first pitch, Jackie made contact, and he sent the pitch soaring far over the left field fence 330 feet away—Robinson had hit a three-run homer. Then Robinson loped around the bases, a smile at last breaking the grim look on his face. When he rounded third, he passed close to his team's manager, a Mississippian who had vigorously opposed a black player on the team. The manager had even said, in all seriousness, that black people were not real human beings. But now the manager looked into Robinson's eyes as he ran by. Then he reached out and gave Robinson a pat on the back.

The players in the dugout stood to greet Robinson. Many of Jackie's teammates gathered around him to pat him on the back or shake his hand. From that very first home run, teammates who had not been sure about how they felt about Jackie were won over. A few would remain cold toward Jackie, but most of Jackie's teammates were glad to have him on their team. "This was the day the dam burst between me and my teammates," Jackie later wrote. "Northerners and Southerners alike, they let me know how much they appreciated the way I had come through."

In the fifth inning, the score was 6–0 with the Royals on top. Robinson laid down a perfect bunt and raced to first ahead of the throw. He stole second and went to third on a groundout. The Giants brought in a relief pitcher, Phil Otis.

Robinson teased him by pretending to be racing to home plate, then stopping and running back to third. On Otis's next windup, Robinson again made a move toward home, causing the pitcher to stop his pitch mid-throw. Immediately, the umpire called a balk—an illegal motion by the pitcher— and Robinson was automatically awarded home. It was dramatic trickery, and the fans loved it! They had never seen such daring base-running as this. The stadium now exploded with screaming, laughing fans, clapping and stamping their feet at the show. Even the Giants fans seemed to share in the amazing moment.

In the seventh inning, Robinson singled sharply, stole another base, and scored on a triple. The Royals' lead jumped to 10–1. In the eighth inning, Robinson bunted his way on base, then scrambled from first to third on an infield hit. His base-running brilliance led the Royals to a 14–1 victory. As soon as the game ended, children streamed from the stands, flowing toward Robinson like a river. Black and white youngsters wanted to get his autograph, or just to touch him. "Color didn't matter to fans," Jackie observed, "if the black man was a winner."

The *Pittsburgh Courier*, in a front-page head-line, said Robinson stole the show in his five trips to the plate. He had gotten four hits, including the three-run home run, scored four times and driven in three runs. He had also stolen two bases.

Joe Bostic, writing in the *Amsterdam News*, said, "Baseball took up the cudgel for democracy and an unassuming, but superlative Negro boy ascended the heights of excellence."

Jackie Robinson had triumphed in his first outing in regular-season organized baseball. But it was only the beginning. He knew he had won an important victory in the first battle, but the war would not be won for a long time. There were many people in baseball who did not want him there, and he knew it. In the weeks and months and even years ahead, there would be moments of humiliation and danger. There would be pitches aimed at his head and spiked shoes cutting into his ankles and shins. There would be spittle on his shoes and the ugliest of racial slurs in his face. There would even be death threats. Robinson knew he would need every ounce of courage and self-control he had in order to endure. But it was going to be worth it. He had made up his mind to be the trailblazer. He was determined to open baseball to a long line of talented young black men who would come after him, men who had been denied their chance before. And he would be the man at the front of the line.

Chapter 2

A Mother's Courage

At six o'clock in the evening on January 31, 1919, Jack Roosevelt Robinson was born near the town of Cairo in Grady County, southern Georgia. He was born in a small cottage owned by his parents, Jerry and Mallie Robinson. When Jack was born, the family already had three sons and a daughter. Mallie had hoped for another girl, but she welcomed her strong-looking baby son with love.

Jack was born at a time when racial segregation was the law in the South. Because he was black, Jack's life would be quite different from a white child's life. From a very early age, it would be made clear to Jack that the color of his skin put him in a lower class. As a result, he would attend an inferior school. He would have to use separate restrooms in town and sit in the back of movie theatres and buses. If he went to a restaurant, he would not be allowed to come in and sit down. The food would be handed to him out the back door.

Worst of all was the constant threat of violence against blacks who dared to challenge this system. And the most terrifying threat came in the form of lynchings. Hundreds of black men, women, and sometimes even children, were tortured and hanged for crimes that, more often than not, they did not even commit. In the year Jack was born, Georgia led the nation in lynchings.

Even so, Mallie Robinson remained strong and hopeful. Because of her optimism, she chose the middle name Roosevelt for her son to honor President Theodore Roosevelt, the 20th president of the United States. Roosevelt had done something no president had ever done before. He said he wanted to open a new era of equality for black Americans. On the night of October 16, 1901, he invited a black man, Booker T. Washington, a famous educator, to the White House for dinner. Many white people were enraged that the president would sit down to dinner with a black man at the White House. Blacks were thrilled. Mallie Robinson was one of them.

Mallie McGriff, one of fourteen children, was the daughter of Wash and Edna McGriff. Mallie's parents were born slaves, and they were freed after the Civil War. But when they had been slaves, it had been against the law for them to learn how to read or write. Therefore, they were very eager for their own children to get an education. Mallie went to school through the sixth grade—an unusual accomplishment for a black girl of that era. Then, as a child, Mallie taught her father to read the Bible. Mallie was raised with strong religious faith and a determination to succeed in life. The McGriffs attended the Rocky Hill African Methodist Church and trusted God to see them through all hardships, including the racism of the time.

Jerry Robinson, Jack's father, was the oldest of eleven children. He worked on a farm and could not read or write. He was a handsome man with great charm, but in many ways he was weak. He was not strong and religious like Mallie.

One Christmas when Mallie was only fourteen years old, she spotted a striking young man at a party who smiled widely at her when their eyes met. Jerry Robinson proceeded to charm the young Mallie. By the end of the party, he had made a date to take her to church the next day. But when Mallie's parents found out that an eighteen-year-old man was dating their fourteen-year-old daughter, they immediately tried to put a stop to it.

Mallie's parents wanted a better husband for their smart and strong-minded daughter. And they had already picked out an educated and upstanding young man from South Carolina. But Mallie craftily pretended to be afraid of this stranger who came from a strange state. While she put on a good act, she continued seeing Jerry. And three years after the Christmas party where they met, Mallie McGriff and Jerry Robinson were married.

The young couple settled in a cabin on a plantation owned by a white man—Jim Sasser. After the Civil War, when the black slaves were freed, many of them continued to work on the plantations where they had been slaves. The difference was that now they got wages, or a share of what they grew. But Mallie quickly learned that this new arrangement was barely better than slavery. While Sasser agreed to give his black workers a share of the vegetables they grew, they had to beg him for everything. And when a hog was slaughtered, Sasser kept nearly all the meat—and even the best bones. The black workers were tossed the fat and scraps.

A strong, independent young woman, Mallie Robinson wanted something better. She insisted that her husband go to Jim Sasser and demand a better deal. After some arguing, Sasser agreed to provide housing, land, fertilizer and seed to the Robinsons in exchange for half of what they produced. This was a much fairer arrangement. It was called sharecropping, and life became better for the Robinsons.

Mallie worked hard, and soon her family had their own hogs, chickens, turkeys and good crops of cotton, peanuts, sugar cane, corn and potatoes.

Life was pretty good, but there was a dark cloud on the horizon. As Mallie would explain forty years later: "We were living as I wanted to live. Only [Jerry's] love was drifting away."

Jerry Robinson liked to party, and he enjoyed flirting with pretty young ladies. And now, thanks mostly to Mallie's hard work, Jerry had money to spend on partying and women. He often went to town looking for excitement, leaving Mallie home to continue doing the work. He also left the family for extended periods. When he came home, his wife always forgave him, but she was growing unhappy. The marriage was beginning to fall apart.

In 1910, the first child, Edgar, was born. Frank was born in 1911, Mack in 1914, Willa Mae in 1916, and Jack in 1919. Jack would be the last child born in the family, because not long after he was born, Jerry Robinson disappeared. Many years later, Jackie discussed what had happened: "Six months after I was born, my father told my mother he was going to visit his brother in Texas . . . My mother was afraid that my father would not come back, and her fears were justified. Later she learned that he had left home and gone away with a neighbor's wife."

It was a terrible blow to Mallie, and the pain she felt also pained Jackie for the rest of his life. "I could only think of him with bitterness," Jackie said. "He had no right to desert my mother and five children." Then, adding insult to injury, Jim Sasser found out that Jerry Robinson was gone, and he evicted Mallie and her children from their home.

Mallie Robinson took a long, hard look at her future, living in the rural South with five children. She could see nothing ahead for her and the children but poverty and misery, and she was determined to find a better future. Also, the tension between blacks and whites was growing worse and worse.

One spring morning, just a few months after Jackie had been born, Mallie heard some chilling news. Not far from where Mallie and the children were living, seven black churches had been burned to the ground. Lynch mobs had gone wild and killed five blacks for no reason at all. Then, only a few weeks later, bloody riots broke out in Charleston, South Carolina. And as spring heated up into summer in the South, lynchings and fires occurred so often that the summer of 1919 became known as "Red Summer." Mallie held her infant son and felt the heat of that summer—she knew it was time to leave.

Burton Thomas, Mallie Robinson's half brother, came to Georgia to visit her during that time. He was well dressed and prosperous-looking. Mallie was impressed. Thomas gave her this advice: "If you want to get closer to heaven, visit California." Thomas lived in southern

California, and he described how very different life was there in a land free from segregation and full of opportunities. Mallie Robinson made up her mind to find a way to go to California, too.

Mallie, her sister Cora Wade, and some other relatives planned to all go together to California. None of them had much money, but by pooling their resources, they thought they could make it. The local white people did not want blacks to leave the area, because they depended on them for cheap labor. They tried in every way to discourage blacks from moving away. But Mallie loaded all her possessions and her children into a buggy and headed for the train station in Cairo. Then Jerry Robinson somehow heard that his wife was leaving town, and he called the police.

When the Robinson family reached the Cairo station, they were met by the police. The policemen poked and prodded the group's suitcases. They asked questions and looked over the train tickets again and again. Mallie tried to remain calm, but her heart was pounding. Sometimes fleeing black families were kicked and beaten. Other times, the police simply tore up the tickets and laughed as the pieces fell to the floor. But these policemen just hassled Mallie Robinson. And she would not back down. At midnight, she and her family boarded train #58.

Mallie sat in the dark, dirty car for black passengers. It would be a long trip sitting on metal seats with five young children. Jack was one year and four months old on May 21, 1920, when they headed out. The oldest child, Edgar, was ten. Mallie Robinson had enough money to get them to California and feed them on the journey, and that was about all. She smoothed out her skirt and smiled to herself, in spite of her worry, as her hand passed over a lumpy wrinkle. Just to be on the safe side, she had sewn all the money she had into her clothes.

Mallie Robinson and her family reached Los Angeles in early June, 1920. The new sights were exciting. She was used to the hills of Georgia, but the towering San Gabriel Mountains and the groves of orange trees amazed her. She called Los Angeles "the most beautiful sight of my whole life." But she did not stay there. She had family in Pasadena, a town about a dozen miles away, and she headed there.

Pasadena was an exotic wonderland of wealth, beautiful rose gardens, and huge stone mansions. But on the other side of the mountains, where the black people lived, it was a different story. The Robinsons' first home was a tiny three-room apartment with no hot water. The walls were dingy, and the kitchen sink was a tin tub. Once she paid the rent, Mallie Robinson had just three dollars left. She had to find work fast.

Twenty-eight-year-old Mallie Robinson went out the first day in search of work. She had to provide her children with food for that day. She left the rundown apartment and found a job as a maid in a white family's home in Pasadena. Mallie was friendly, obviously sincere, and a hard worker, so she had no trouble finding work. Her pay was eight dollars a week, and the hours were good. Back in Georgia she had worked from sunup to sundown, but here she was off work at 4:00 in the afternoon. Being finished with work so early seemed strange to Mallie—so strange, in fact, that she sought out evening cooking jobs in order to bring in a little more money. Jackie remembered that he rarely saw his mother during this time because she was working late into the night to support the family: "She was hands caressing us or a voice in our sleep."

When Mallie's first job ended because the family moved, she quickly found another with the Dodge family in Pasadena. She worked for them for the next twenty years.

After several weeks in the apartment, Mallie Robinson and her sister and her family moved in with half-brother Burton Thomas, whose glowing tales of California had brought them here. Thomas had a nice house with a large backyard at 45 Glorieta Street, a tree-lined street in Pasadena. A few black families were living in this mostly white neighborhood. California did not have housing segregation, although many of the deeds were written to prevent blacks from owning homes in certain neighborhoods. Even in California, however, where laws did not keep blacks from white areas, public pressure often did. When a white family showed signs of selling their home to a black family, neighbors would pressure them to change their minds.

Pasadena had a mixed attitude toward black people. It was far more tolerant of blacks than the South was, but in one way this was harder on some blacks. They knew where they stood in the South, but they never could be sure in Pasadena. Incidents of racial hatred would spring up at unexpected times. In 1909 whites tried to burn down a black church in Pasadena because they saw it as a drawing card for more blacks to move there.

When the Pasadena City Council opened the only municipal pool in Pasadena—the Brookside Plunge—they restricted its use to whites only. When black people protested, they relented by allowing blacks to use the pool one day a week, calling it "International Day." In an insulting decision by the Council, however, whites were assured that after the blacks had their swimming day, the pool would be drained and fresh water would be pumped in.

Mallie Robinson saved her money and eventually was able to buy a home for her family. She found a two-story white house on Pepper Street in Pasadena. It was an old post office converted to a house with five bedrooms and two bathrooms. The house was nicknamed "the Castle" because it was a better place than the Robinsons had ever known before. Many fruit trees had been planted in the yard, including apples, oranges, peaches, and figs. Mallie Robinson made sure the fruit was eaten in season or put up in jars for the off-season. She did not waste anything. She also planted a garden filled with bright flowers and vegetables. She wanted her children to be able to go outside and pick vegetables from the garden, even though they lived in the city.

The house was in a mostly white neighborhood, and some of the neighbors were not pleased by black people on the street. A few angry neighbors attempted to buy out the home from the Robinsons, but they didn't have enough money. The only neighbor with enough money was an elderly widow who lived next door. But Mallie was kind and generous to her widowed neighbor. She sent her older sons over to help with chores and also sent over flowers and treats. Before long, the elderly neighbor was a good friend.

Ten-year-old Edgar and nine-year-old Frank began school at Grover Cleveland Elementary School. Unlike in the South, here black and white children attended school together in the same schools. But the school the Robinson boys attended was primarily white. In general, the house at 121 Pepper Street became a very good place for Mallie Robinson and her children.

Ducks, chickens, pigeons and rabbits also lived at the Pepper Street address. There were five hungry children, and by growing and raising much of their own food in the summer, Mallie Robinson did not have to spend as much of her modest income on food. Still, in later years Jackie Robinson recalled times when there was not enough to go around, and at times there were only two meals a day at the Robinson house. Sometimes Mallie was able to bring leftovers home from her job. But now and then the family had to make a meal of stale bread and water mixed with sugar.

One night, not long after the Robinsons had moved to Pepper Street, they awoke to see a cross in flames in their front yard. The racists of the South often used this strategy to frighten the local black people. And some of the racist people on Pepper Street were certain that it would scare a single mother with five children. But Mallie Robinson was strong, and she would not be scared off. Finally, when the angry white neighbors could not buy Mallie out or scare her off, they resorted to the lowest form of pressure. They decided to pick on Mallie's children instead. And it was during this time that Jackie Robinson would have his first personal experience with racism.

Chapter 3

The Fatherless Boy

Edgar Robinson loved to roller-skate down the sidewalk on his street. The sound of wheels on concrete annoyed some neighbors, especially those hoping the Robinsons would leave. The police were called often to the house on Pepper Street. They told Mallie Robinson that her son was making too much noise. They advised her to keep her children in the house.

Before long, the police were coming every other day to the Robinson house. Mallie refused to cave in to this new form of harassment by a handful of racist neighbors. Her active boys were making no more noise than any other youngsters their age. Jackie Robinson later recalled, "Pasadena regarded us as intruders. My brothers and I were in many a fight that started with a racial slur on the very street we lived on."

While stubbornly resisting attempts to force her children off the street and deny them normal outdoor activity, Mallie Robinson would not tolerate retaliation against the white neighbors either. Once, Edgar and his friends decided to spread tar on the lawn of the neighbor doing most of the complaining. Mallie Robinson marched her son and his friends to the damaged lawn and stood grim watch as they cleaned the grass with rags soaked in kerosene and then painstakingly clipped the blades that could not be cleaned.

When Jackie Robinson was very small, he was deeply attached to his mother. He wanted to be with her all the time, even to the point of wanting to sleep in her downstairs bedroom. He did not want to join his siblings in the upstairs bedroom. It troubled Jackie to have his mother going off to work each day, and he wanted to make the most of the time he did have with her. Mallie Robinson even promised Jackie twenty-five cents a week to move upstairs, but for a long time he refused.

While Mallie worked, Jackie was cared for by his sister, Willa Mae, who became a second mother to him. Just two years older than Jackie, she dressed and fed her little brother. When Willa Mae started kindergarten, there was no one to leave Jackie with, so she took him along. At first, the teacher was not happy having a three-year-old in the classroom, and he sent a note home to Mallie letting her know that Jackie would have to stay at home. But that night, Mallie taught Jackie to say, "Good morning, Teacher" and smile politely.

Eventually, the teacher was won over. A

sandbox was placed outside the classroom window so that Willa Mae could both do her own schoolwork and keep an eye on Jackie. Looking back on that year, Jackie would later comment, "Everyone was very nice to me; however, I was certainly very happy when, after a year of living in a sandbox, I became old enough to go to school."

Jackie Robinson was a handsome and smart little boy, but he had a streak of mischief. When Jackie was finally old enough to leave the sandbox and attend school, he decided to play a trick on his classmates. A nearby tree dropped acorns, which he carefully collected. As the children were coming to school in the morning, he pelted them with the acorns, and for quite some time they were unsure where the attack was coming from.

However, one afternoon when Jackie was about eight years old, his first personal experience with racism would anger him enough to throw something harder than acorns. Looking back on the incident, Jackie remembered it this way: "I was sweeping our sidewalk when a little neighbor girl shouted at me, 'Nigger, nigger, nigger!' I was old enough to know how to answer that. I had learned from my older brother that the most insulting name you can call a white person is 'cracker.' This is what I called her."

Within seconds, the little girl's father stormed outside and began screaming at young Jackie.

Then it got even worse. "I don't remember who threw the first stone," Jackie recalled, "but the father and I had a pretty good stone-throwing fight going until the girl's mother came out and made him go back into the house."

It was Mallie Robinson's kind spirit that eventually won over even the most hostile white neighbors. To help her own family, Robinson made a deal with a local bakery. At the end of the day, the bakery usually threw away the slightly stale but still good products. They agreed to deliver them instead to the Robinson house. Jackie's mother wrapped cookies and pastries in boxes and had her children take them to the meanest neighbors. Truly, by loving her enemies, Mallie eventually softened the anger that these neighbors felt.

But being a good neighbor was not Mallie's only skill. Although Mallie Robinson worked as a maid, her many amazing qualities went far beyond her humble job. She had a bright, bubbly personality, and she enjoyed spinning tales. She even acted out the various roles in a story. She was always ready to do something new and different. When someone brought a horse down Pepper Street, Mallie decided to try to ride the horse, and off she galloped to the amusement of her children. "I thought she must have some kind of magic to do all the things she did," Jackie said of his mother.

Mallie Robinson gave her children strong values. In the Robinson household, there was never a gray area between right and wrong. She taught the children that God was a living presence always nearby. Every night, the whole family prayed on their knees. God was comforter and guide, Mallie Robinson believed. Her value system put God at the top, followed by family, education, and self-control.

Mallie Robinson was generous, especially to family members. When any of them wanted to escape Georgia for the kinder world of California, she was ready with a helping hand. When her father died, she took her mother, Edna McGriff, into the family home. She would not hear of anything else.

Jackie Robinson later spoke of what a powerful impact his grandmother had on him. "I remember sitting by the flickering light of an oil lantern," Jackie recalled, "and watching her face, which had a thousand wrinkles in it." Jackie was fascinated by both his grandmother's face and her life. She taught young Jackie, far better than any books could have, what it was like to be a slave. She told the boy that as he went through life, he must never allow bigoted white people to make him feel less than the proud, fine person that he was. On July 25, 1933, when Jackie was fourteen, his grandmother died, but he never forgot her lessons. She brought home to Jackie

Robinson that he was the son of sharecroppers and the grandson of slaves, but that did not lower him in any way.

In 1924, Jackie Robinson started school at Cleveland Elementary School. All the teachers were white, but there were other black children. Jackie liked his teachers, and they were kind to him. Often some of the children, including Jackie, had come to school hungry, so the teachers made them sandwiches. Jackie grew very close to his teachers, and they remained his friends throughout his life.

Though school segregation did not exist in Pasadena, there was an underlying racism. Most white teachers coming into the profession preferred to teach at schools with all-white student bodies. Most black parents had a feeling their children were not being treated equally, though Mallie Robinson was pleased at how well her children got along at school.

In 1926, the area was rezoned, and Jackie attended Washington Elementary School. In 1931, twelve-year-old Jackie began attending Washington Junior High School. He usually earned B's and C's in his classes. He was a bright youngster but enjoyed athletics more than studying. His teachers at Washington Junior High wrote on his file that he would make a good gardener.

Even as a young child, Jackie loved games.

"He was a special little boy," his sister Willa Mae said. "Ever since I can remember, he always had a ball in his hand." And though Jackie's mother put education before sports, she recognized and encouraged her young son's love of games. Poor as they were, there was no money for any kind of ball or sports equipment. But Mallie found a way around that. One morning, Jackie found his mother unraveling some old wool socks and winding the wool into a tight ball. Then, after covering the wool with material, Mallie handed Jackie his first ball. All Jackie had to do was find a strong stick, and he was all set for batting practice.

From baseball to marbles to soccer, Jackie had a powerful desire to win, no matter what he was playing. He was good with a ball, and he rarely lost. When Jackie reached junior high, the students played a game in which they all gathered in a circle and dodged a thrown ball. Jackie was always the winner. In junior high, athletic skill was more important than the race and economic class someone came from. So Jackie became very popular with his white and Asian-American classmates. The boys all competed against each other in a spirit of friendliness. At a young age, Jackie Robinson was part of integrated sports, and he enjoyed the experience.

In the early 1930s, when Jackie was in his teens, the United States was in the midst of a serious economic crisis. The Great Depression, as it was called, led to people losing their jobs, their homes, and their farms. White and black families all suffered, but the blacks suffered more because they had less to begin with. In Pasadena, some of the wealthy white families could no longer afford black servants, so blacks lost their jobs. When they did keep their jobs, they often had to take a pay cut. Mallie Robinson, now nearing forty, was the only wage earner in her family at 121 Pepper Street. The five Robinson children lived there, as well as son Frank's wife and his two children. Often, other needy relatives were there too, and Mallie Robinson was feeding them all. Because she was such an excellent maid, she kept her job.

Jackie felt sorry for his hard-working mother. "My pride in my mother was tempered with a sense of sadness that she had to bear most of our burdens," Jackie said. "At a very early age I began to want to relieve her in any small way I could. I was happy whenever I had money I could give to her." So he took all the part-time jobs he could find, from delivering newspapers to mowing the neighbors' lawns to selling hot dogs during games at the nearby Rose Bowl. But as much as Jackie loved helping his mother, he often hated all this extra work because it took time from his studies. His grades began slipping. He loved reading and often checked books out of the library, but now he had no time for reading, either.

Pressures were building in young Jackie Robinson. He knew he was poorer than most of his classmates. His family did not have the things their families had. Jackie pretended it did not matter, but sometimes he felt inferior because of it. Worst of all, Jackie was feeling the lack of a father in his life. He was just a baby when his parents separated, and he had no contact with his father. The Robinsons were not even sure what had happened to Jerry Robinson. Word came to Mallie when Jackie was a toddler that Jerry Robinson had died, but she never knew for sure.

Mallie always avoided criticizing her husband to the children. She did not want to poison their image of him, but the older children had already formed opinions. Jackie's brother Edgar remembered a man who was ready to whip him over the slightest misdeed. Jackie's sister, Willa Mae, said later that she did not need a father, but Jackie Robinson missed the father he never knew. A cousin who was close to Jackie recalled that Jackie was frequently annoyed by not having enough to eat or embarrassed by having only old clothes. "But I think he was really unhappy because he didn't have a father," the cousin concluded. Indeed, being a fatherless boy cast a shadow over Jackie's young life.

Chapter 4

The Four-Sport Star

As Jackie Robinson grew into his middle teens, he felt keenly that his father had betrayed him and the family. He was not there for them when they needed him. Jackie understood how hard it was to be a black man in Georgia fighting racism and poverty. He knew that a man's spirit could be damaged. But still he could not forgive his missing father.

All during the years of being alone, Mallie Robinson never considered marrying again. Even when she was fairly sure Jerry Robinson was dead, she did not want to take the chance of giving her children a bad stepfather. She could not have stood seeing the children mistreated. So though she was only in her twenties when she became single, she spent the rest of her life without a husband.

As Jackie Robinson matured, his happy, charming nature changed. He turned shy and reserved. He felt he could only truly be himself in his tight little circle of close friends. He wanted nothing to do with girls, though he was a handsome young man. One day, the prettiest girl in Jackie's class approached him just to talk. Secretly, Jackie had a crush on this girl, but he was so nervous and confused that he actually told her to "go jump in a lake." Later he confessed to not knowing how to act around girls.

Jackie looked up to his older brothers to find role models, but he was frustrated. His eldest brother, Edgar, had a strange personality that Jackie could never quite understand. Edgar was in love with speed, and actually received a speeding ticket one time for going too fast on his skates. Edgar also performed dangerous and frightening feats on his bicycle, jumping over the hoods of cars and racing a city bus for thirty miles. Then he got a motorcycle and rode it so fast that his family took it away from him. He quit school in sixth grade, but he was already a good reader. He enjoyed reading and quoting from the Bible. It appeared to outsiders that Edgar may have suffered from some form of mental illness. At that time such things were not diagnosed in many cases, and Edgar lived his entire life as a loner. Jackie was troubled by Edgar's condition and later admitted, "There was always something about him that was mysterious to me."

Brother Frank was a good-natured boy, tall and slender and a favorite with the girls. Frank and Jackie were very close. "He was always there to protect me when I was in a [fight]," Jackie remembered, "even though I don't think he could knock down a fly." Still, as charming and successful in school as Frank was, he soon found out that his skin color would keep him from getting a good job. He eventually settled on being a tree trimmer. Even after he married, he could not afford his own home, so he brought his family home to his mother. But through it all, Frank was very dear to Jackie, surely his closest sibling.

Brother Mack was four and a half years older than Jackie, and he was the one who became Jackie's hero. Mack was a star athlete in Pasadena, and his triumphs introduced Jackie to the shining world of sports glory, a world he wanted to be a part of himself. Jackie went to track meets with Mack, and he joined in the cheering crowd when Mack would win meets. Mack was a great sprinter, especially in the over-200 meters (220 yards) competitions.

Mack's racing style was exciting. Jackie would watch his older brother nervously as the other runners would blast out at the start and instantly pull ahead of Mack. But Jackie knew what was coming. Right when he needed it, Mack would suddenly put on an incredible burst of speed and fly past every other runner to win the race.

With a talent like Mack's, qualifying for the 1936 Olympics in Berlin, Germany was a real possibility. And even though Mack was diagnosed with a heart condition, he worked hard and focused on his dream. When 1936 came, Jackie was proud to let everyone know that his brother's dream had indeed come true—he would be competing in the Olympics.

In Germany, the tyrant Adolf Hitler had been telling the world that only white athletes had the strength and skill to win medals. The great Jesse Owens and Mack Robinson would prove Hitler wrong in the 1936 Olympics. Back in Pasadena, the Robinson family gathered around the radio to hear the results. Jackie was seventeen when he heard that his brother, Mack, had won the silver medal in the 200-meter dash, finishing less than half a second behind Jesse Owens, who took the gold. And in another race, Mack Robinson set a world record.

When Mack returned to Pasadena, he thought he would be the hometown hero, but no one seemed to care about his silver medal. And while white athletes returning from the Olympics were offered coaching and broadcasting jobs, Jesse Owens was reduced to racing against horses like a circus act. Similarly, the best job Mack could get was working nights sweeping the streets. When he wore his Olympic jacket at work, people complained that he was not showing respect for the Olympics. But the jacket was the only warm coat Mack Robinson owned, and the nights were chilly. He had to wear it.

As he grew older, Jackie depended more on his friends for companionship and less on his brothers. Jackie had a group of male friends who became known as the "Pepper Street Gang." Members included his cousin, friends from elementary school, and neighbors. They were black, Japanese-American, Mexican-American, and white.

Nobody seriously feared the Pepper Street Gang would turn to serious crime, but they were often an unruly and troublesome bunch of boys. There was little gang activity in Pasadena, and the Pepper Street Gang limited itself to fairly harmless activities such as throwing dirt at cars and stealing fruit from a local market. Jackie was more interested in mischief than in crime.

One of the gang's favorite pastimes was stealing balls off of golf courses before the golfers could find where their balls had landed. Jackie and his friends hid behind the trees, snickering at the baffled golfers who swore and stomped around when they couldn't find their golf balls. However, one time Jackie got caught. The golfer was angry, but he made a deal with Jackie. If Jackie could putt the ball to the hole in fewer strokes than the golfer, Jackie could keep the ball and win a dollar. But if he lost, he would be in trouble. Jackie focused his steely eyes on the ball and awkwardly gripped the putter. He had never played golf before, but he was determined to win—not so much for the dollar and the ball, but because he couldn't stand to lose. Five minutes later, the golfer was shaking his head and pulling out his wallet to pay Jackie.

Even though the Pepper Street Gang was far from dangerous, it was not long before their antics attracted the attention of the police department.

And one day, Jackie Robinson committed the most serious crime of the Gang when he jumped into the city reservoir for an illegal swim. Jackie thought it was unjust that black youths like himself were banned from the Brookside Plunge because of the color of their skin, so he decided to swim elsewhere, ignoring the signs. Jackie later described the police surrounding the reservoir and shouting, "Look there, a nigger swimming in my drinking water!" After being taunted, Jackie was taken to jail at gunpoint. He got off with a warning, but soon police were coming regularly to Mallie Robinson's door to complain about Jackie.

Jackie Robinson admitted later that he may well have been on the road to juvenile delinquency. He had no father to guide him, and he was resentful of racial slights. He was hanging with a group of friends who were often looking for trouble. What turned Jackie around completely was a man named Carl Anderson. A black auto mechanic just seven years older than Jackie, he worked at a corner where the Pepper Street Gang often hung around. Anderson worked to advance equality in Pasadena and help teenagers. When the local Boy Scouts refused to admit blacks, he started the first black Boy Scout troop in northwest Pasadena. He also organized a black social group called "The Friendly Indians."

Jackie and his friends enjoyed visiting with Anderson and looking into engines. Anderson talked to Jackie Robinson as a big brother or father would. "He made me see that if I continued with the gang, it would hurt my mother as well as myself," Jackie recalled. "He said that it didn't take guts to follow the crowd, that courage lay in being willing to be different." Jackie thought long and hard about all the sacrifices his mother had made for him and how hurting her would be more painful than anything he could imagine. "I was too ashamed to tell Carl how right he was," Jackie admitted, "but what he said got to me." And soon, Jackie found the courage to be different.

But even with his newfound courage, Jackie Robinson was often hurt and angered by the racism he constantly ran into. Simply because of his skin color, he could not join the YMCA, get waited on in a restaurant, or sit in a good seat at the movies. He never showed his anger, but it was always there. He remained calm on the outside and burned inside. Jackie was not an explosive person. He never rebelled against his family, and he never used profanity in the house. When Jackie was totally furious, the worst term he would use was "dadgummit."

Another person who helped turn Jackie away from trouble and deal with his anger was Karl Downs, the young pastor at Mallie Robinson's church. Downs was not like any minister Jackie had ever met before. He played basketball and baseball and liked a lot of spirited music during his church services. Sometimes Downs's behavior annoyed the older members of the church, but Downs didn't care—he was after the souls of the young.

Pastor Downs got Jackie Robinson back into the habit of regular churchgoing. Downs led the young man to accept Christ, and he also provided a caring ear to hear some of Robinson's problems. Robinson continued to be troubled by his mother's hard life. Her work did not seem to lead to rewards for her. But Downs helped Robinson to see how by giving so much love to her family and others, Mallie Robinson was a great success, and her unselfish love would inspire Jackie Robinson to make great strides in life.

In 1935, Jackie Robinson enrolled at John Muir Technical High School, a school with a great sports program. It would become the first stage that would display the athletic talents of Jackie Robinson to the outside world.

Sixteen-year-old Jackie Robinson was tall, but he weighed just 135 pounds, making him fast and nimble. And after a year at Muir, Jackie was starring in all sports—baseball, football, basketball, and track. First of all, Jackie fell in love with the broad jump, describing it this way: "You jump—you really try to jump off the earth, and your legs churn the air like you want to reach the moon." Next, in the fall of 1936, Jackie Robinson shone in football, becoming the star player on the team. At a packed game held at the Rose Bowl, Robinson scored a rushing touchdown in the final minutes of the game, leading Muir to victory. The Pasadena Post put a large photo of Robinson on the front page of the sports section. Though he cracked his ribs in a later game, Robinson was an electrifying quarterback who gave Muir a great season.

With his ribs healed, it was back to basketball for Robinson. He now had reached a height of six feet, and he led the Muir team to victory after victory. On January 29, 1937, eighteen-year-old Jackie Robinson played an incredible game. It was Muir against archrival Glendale for first place. And since, as a senior, it would be Jackie's last game, he played with everything he had. A local newspaper, the *Pasadena Post*, described his effort that night: "Robinson was all over the floor, and when he wasn't scoring points he was making impossible 'saves' and interceptions, and was the best player on the floor." The Terriers won that night, thanks to Jackie. It was a sweet way to end the season.

Robinson had loved the school and had enjoyed playing here. His teammates felt the same about him. Another paper, the *Pasadena Star-News,* which was not always favorable to black players, declared Robinson as the outstanding Muir athlete, a standout in football, basketball, track, baseball and even tennis.

Jackie Robinson enrolled at Pasadena Junior College, where he would gain even more recognition in his four top sports. The dynamic young athlete would attract the attention of national sportswriters. Robinson blossomed at Pasadena City College. He said later, "It was there that I lost most of my shyness."

When Jackie Robinson arrived at PJC, his brother Mack was already a student there. They were among the sixty to seventy black students in a student body of four thousand, but the college was mostly relaxed and friendly when it came to race relations. All classes, swimming facilities, and social events were open to everyone. The only exception was dance class; blacks and whites were not allowed to dance together.

Jackie continued to be a bit of a loner, not making friends easily. But one night he was standing around with a group of other black students who seemed as shy and bored as he was. Suddenly, a short young man who looked familiar to Jackie, shouted out, "Anybody around here going to have some waffles?" The question was met with complete silence, but Jackie took a chance and answered, "Did I hear you mention waffles? Let's go!"

From that point on, the short young man, Jack Gordon, and Jackie became inseparable best friends. They had been on rival football teams during high school, occasionally taunting one another, but that was in the past. Now Gordon showed Jackie how to meet girls and even set him up on his first date with, by sheer chance, the same girl that Jackie had told to "go jump in a lake" years earlier! That, too, was in the past, and Jackie soon discovered that he enjoyed dating and was no longer painfully shy around girls.

But Jackie Robinson's first love was still sports—all sports. First, he joined the baseball team, the Bulldogs, and his leadership gave the team the most successful season in PJC history. Then he became the college's second best broad jumper, right behind brother Mack. Jackie and Mack often found themselves competing directly against each other, but the rivalry never became bitter or angry. "I always had the greatest respect for Mack," Jackie explained.

Robinson then turned to Bulldog football at Pasadena Junior College. He displayed amazing skill and was nicknamed the "dashing quarterback" because of his ability to both pass and run the football. He was rapidly becoming a school hero, but socially he remained with his small group of black friends.

Although Robinson was well-liked at the school, he still continued to be humiliated and angered by racist treatment. When the Bulldogs went on tour, Robinson began to experience what he would eventually have to face on a daily basis. The team was in Sacramento, and when they entered a restaurant, Robinson and the other blacks were refused service. In Phoenix, the team tried to register at a nice hotel, but the desk clerk refused to give rooms to the black players and told them to go elsewhere. Sent to a small, dingy hotel, the black players were so angry that they refused to take the rooms. Instead they sat in the lobby all night, talking quietly and trying to sleep in uncomfortable chairs.

Jackie Robinson often acted as peacemaker when there was racial trouble. When white players on the Bulldog team were giving Robinson's black teammates the cold shoulder, Robinson did not get angry. Instead, he talked to the white players in a friendly way, telling them that both blacks and whites had the same number of good and bad qualities, and racial divisions hurt everybody. Robinson had long ago learned from his mother's kindness toward racist neighbors on Pepper Street that losing one's temper achieved nothing. It only brought more trouble.

But when the Bulldogs played Long Beach Junior College, Jackie finally did lose his temper.

There had been advance warning that there would be trouble—so much warning that Mack Robinson arrived armed with a tire iron. When the game was over, a substitute guard for Long Beach walked over and punched Jackie Robinson. Jackie punched the other man back, and a major battle broke out involving players, coaches, and fans. Later, the Long Beach student-body president apologized to Robinson and the Bulldogs, who had won not only the game, but also the fight.

A few days later, on January 22nd, Jackie Robinson got into serious trouble. Robinson and a friend were coming from a movie theatre, and the friend was singing a then popular song, "Flat Foot Floogie," just as the pair passed a police officer. The officer felt the mocking song was aimed at him personally, and he confronted the two young black men. Both black men were arrested. Robinson spent the night in a Pasadena city jail, the police not allowing him to call his mother or a friend. At his hearing, Robinson was sentenced to ten days in jail, but since he had never been arrested before and he was a football star, the sentence was suspended. He was put on probation for two years and told if he got in trouble before that time, he would be forced to serve the ten-day sentence.

The incident did not appear in the newspapers, but it was known in Pasadena. It led to a flurry of ugly rumors that Robinson was violent and antisocial. Many believed the lie that Jackie was constantly in and out of jail and that he was only released to play football. The truth was that Robinson never looked for trouble, but if he was attacked, he fought back.

By the fall of 1938, Jackie Robinson at nineteen was a 175-pounder with broad shoulders, heavy thighs, and a full six feet of height. He was an impressive-looking young athlete. He held a broad-jump record, and he had excelled in football, basketball and baseball. He was honored as the greatest all-around athlete to ever attend Pasadena Junior College.

Forty thousand fans watched undefeated Pasadena beat Compton, highlighted by a dazzling display of football magic by Jackie Robinson. He caught the ball after the kickoff, reversed field three times, and returned the kickoff for a touchdown. In San Francisco, before another huge crowd, Robinson came through with a seventy-five-yard run for a touchdown. On Homecoming Day in November against Glendale in the Rose Bowl, Robinson made an eighty-five-yard sprint that helped ensure a 33–6 victory.

Jackie Robinson was becoming a sensation. In his last game as a Bulldog, he caught a punt deep in the end zone and raced 104 yards for another touchdown, stunning Caltech. Robinson led the Bulldogs to an 11–0 season. He had scored 17 touchdowns and 131 points. Bulldogs' coach

Mallory called Robinson a "gift from heaven."

After Robinson's incredible accomplishments at Pasadena Junior College, sports departments at universities all over the country were talking about this amazing Jackie Robinson. This was an athlete who could make a sports program come alive. Offers of scholarships poured in. One coach from a northern California school even offered to arrange a scholarship for Jackie to a school in the East if Jackie did not want to accept his offer. When Jackie asked why, the coach explained that he didn't want his team to have to compete against a team Jackie was on. But with the counsel of his brother, Frank, Jackie Robinson chose the University of California in Los Angeles, UCLA. The tuition was free, and Robinson could live at home while commuting to the college's Westwood campus.

Jackie Robinson was a highly respected superstar, but there would soon be an ugly reminder that even in Pasadena, the color of a man's skin could mean everything. In January, Edgar Robinson was stopped by a police officer along the Tournament of Roses parade route for setting up chairs for the parade watchers to rent. But Edgar explained that he had just paid four dollars for a special license that allowed him to rent chairs. Slowly, he reached in his pocket to pull out the license. That was a mistake. Believing he might be reaching for a weapon, the officer knocked Edgar Robinson down. What followed is confusing, but Edgar ended up with a black eye and twisted and bruised arms.

Edgar was taken to jail and not permitted to call home. Although beaten and in pain, he was given no access to medical care. Confused and afraid, Edgar pleaded guilty to charges of resisting arrest and placing chairs illegally on the sidewalk. After paying a ten-dollar fine, he was freed. He went to a city hospital seeking treatment and was turned away. Edgar then went to the chief of police to protest what had happened to him, but he was told by the chief himself to get out before he was clubbed on the head. When the Pasadena branch of the NAACP protested the brutal treatment of this obviously impaired man, it was ignored. The incident embittered Jackie Robinson and strengthened his feelings that even after all his athletic triumphs, he and his family were not completely welcome in Pasadena. "If my mother, brothers, and sister weren't living there, I'd never go back," Jackie had angrily said. "People in Pasadena were less understanding, in some ways, than Southerners."

In February 1939, just after his twentieth birthday, Jackie Robinson began attending classes at UCLA. He drove a 1931 Plymouth to school. At first he decided not to be a four-sport star because he needed more time to study; UCLA was a difficult school, but Jackie was determined to do well. He chose to focus on football and the broad jump only. Like his brother Mack, Jackie dreamed of making the Olympic team and competing in the broad jump.

Jackie Robinson was earning good grades and enjoying school. He was even playing a little tennis. To his surprise, he won the men's singles and doubles titles in the 10th Annual Championship Tournament of the Black Western Federation of Tennis clubs. A natural at nearly any sport, Jackie had barely focused on tennis and still became a champion.

Jackie Robinson had come to a good place in his life. But one spring morning in 1939, Jackie would receive a phone call that would shatter that good place and break the hearts of everyone in his family.

Chapter 5

The Soldier and the Nurse

The night of July 10, 1939, Frank Robinson was riding his motorcycle on Orange Grove Avenue when a car coming from the opposite direction swerved into his path to enter a service station. Frank Robinson braked and desperately tried to avoid the collision. But the left front fender of the car crashed into him. Robinson and a passenger riding behind him on the motorcycle were both hurled into the air. The passenger was not seriously injured, but Robinson struck a parked car and was knocked unconscious. He was taken to Huntington Memorial Hospital suffering from a fractured skull, broken ribs, leg and thigh, as well as internal injuries to his liver, spleen, kidney and lung.

Jackie Robinson had been at a friend's house playing cards when he received the call from the hospital. He was told his brother was dying. Crushed with grief, Jackie went home and collapsed sobbing on his bed. Mallie Robinson went to the hospital and remained at her son's bedside until he died around midnight. Jackie was stunned: "It was hard to believe he was gone—hard to believe I would no longer have his support."

Jackie Robinson grieved long and hard for Frank. Later he would dedicate athletic triumphs to his older brother. Jackie would always miss the love and support he got from the brother he had been closest to. As a way to deal with his sorrow, Jackie focused on sports and competition with even greater energy and with a burning desire to win, always win, in memory of Frank.

Then, not even two months after the death of his brother, Jackie found himself in the middle of another ugly confrontation fueled by racism. On September 5, 1939, Jackie Robinson and his friends were returning from a softball game. A couple of friends were riding on the running board of Robinson's Plymouth, and everybody was in good spirits. Then, apparently irritated by seeing a group of young black men having fun, a white motorist passed by and yelled racial slurs at the group. Robinson and the white driver stopped, and soon there was a yelling match. A passing motorcycle officer noticed the crowd of mostly young blacks milling around, and he saw trouble. When the officer stopped, many of the young black men fled, but Jackie Robinson remained there, refusing to run away or hide. Robinson remembered that "I found myself up against the side of my car with a gun barrel pressed unsteadily into the pit of my stomach. I was scared to death."

Robinson was arrested on charges of resisting arrest and blocking traffic. He was taken to jail and denied his request to call home. He was placed in a cell, where he remained until the next morning when he pleaded not guilty. The case was scheduled for September 19, and Robinson was freed on a twenty-five-dollar bond.

The incident would not have been serious except for the earlier suspended jail sentence from 1938. If Robinson were found guilty on this new charge, then he could be forced to spend a month in jail for not keeping out of trouble for two years. When word reached UCLA that its promising athlete was in danger of going to jail, the university put pressure on the court, and the case was quickly settled. Jackie had mixed feelings about this incident. He was relieved that his value as an athlete had kept him out of jail. But he was very angry to endure horrible treatment simply because he was black. And he was well aware of what would have happened if he had not been important to the university as an athlete.

In 1939, UCLA obviously allowed black students to attend the university, but it wasn't exactly encouraged. As a result, out of 9,600 students at UCLA, only about fifty were black. In addition, it was very hard for the black students at

UCLA to find housing or get hired for part-time jobs on campus. And it was even more difficult for black students to be included in social events. It was clearly understood that they were not to attend parties with white students, so the tiny group of blacks socialized among themselves.

Still, UCLA welcomed Jackie Robinson because he was a great athlete and the university was desperately in need of star power on the field. UCLA was a fairly new school when Jackie arrived, but it was in the same sports division as older, stronger colleges like USC, Berkeley, Stanford and Oregon. UCLA was the new kid on the block and needed some victories. It hoped Jackie Robinson would help.

Jackie Robinson joined the Bruins, UCLA's football team, as a running back. He joined Kenny Washington, another black player, already there, and the great Woody Strode, who would later become a movie star. UCLA saw the dynamic young black athletes as the key to their sports future. Robinson, Washington and Strode were nicknamed "The Gold Dust Trio" for the luster they were expected to add to the Bruins.

On a night in late September, 65,000 fans crowded into the Los Angeles Coliseum, UCLA's home field, for the opening of the football season. All-white Texas Christian University had come to play them. The TCU Frogs were the top ranked team in the country, and they fully expected to keep it that way. They thought they would hardly work up a sweat in defeating UCLA.

When the Bruins took the field, Washington and Robinson led the attack. UCLA won, with the TCU center ruefully saying, "We've never run into anything like [Washington and Robinson], and I hope never to again." The following week the Bruins won over the University of Washington 14–7 in Seattle. Robinson was hailed as the hero of the game when he returned a punt 65 yards to the Huskies' 5-yard line. He dazzled the fans with his hard-charging style of play, even those from Washington, and at the end of the game, he got a standing ovation from everyone in the stadium.

Against Stanford the next week, the Bruins were on the brink of losing when Jackie Robinson, now playing safety, jumped three feet off the ground, intercepted the ball, and ran 50 yards to score and tie the game. This earned Robinson a new nickname, "Jack Rabbit Jack." With blinding speed and tricky footwork, Robinson was leading the Bruins to unimagined heights of glory. When Robinson joined the Bruins, they expected good things from him, but they never dared hope for this.

At the final game of the season, UCLA was undefeated with two ties. They were now playing USC for the Pacific Coast championship and a place in the Rose Bowl. A record-setting crowd of 103,352 spectators sat on the edge of their seats through the entire game. A mighty roar thundered through the stadium when a tackle by Jackie caused the only fumble of USC's entire season. Still, the game ended in a tie, and because USC had all wins and no ties on their record, they went to the Rose Bowl. But not one UCLA fan was disappointed with that magical season.

Sadly, Robinson and Washington were ignored when post-season honors were given. And even among his teammates, Jackie Robinson was resented for the attention he was getting in the sports press. When an article appeared in the *Bruin* declaring Robinson a better football player than the great white star Red Grange, some white readers were irate.

But even though Jackie's stunning season was mostly ignored once it was over, the UCLA boosters club, at least, decided to reward him. Made up of alumni who were hungry for just such an exciting season as Robinson had provided, they gave Robinson a Model A Ford to replace his old Plymouth. Gifts like this would later be illegal from booster clubs to players, but in 1939 they were common. Jackie Robinson welcomed the car and felt grateful that he was appreciated.

Jackie Robinson was enjoying his success at UCLA, but he was lonely and often withdrawn. Some people saw him as a sullen and unfriendly loner, but that reputation was probably not fair. After all, Robinson was still in mourning for his brother. And Jackie's dislike of drinking, partying, and chasing women had more to do with his own morals than with being "unfriendly." Also, the atmosphere at UCLA was strange for a young man who had been comfortable in his old neighborhood with friends he had known since childhood.

Along with his classes and sports, Robinson worked two jobs while a student at UCLA. He was an assistant janitor, and he worked at an off-campus book store—Campbell's. The store was run by a couple who liked to hire black students and had once employed Ralph Bunche when he was a star basketball player at UCLA. Later Bunche became a diplomat and Nobel Peace Prize winner for his efforts in resolving world conflicts. The Campbells, who were white, developed a close friendship with Jackie Robinson, and when the Bruin football banquet was held, they insisted on Mallie Robinson sitting at their table.

During the summer of 1940, Jackie spent the months playing golf and tennis when he was not working at Warner Brothers in the property department. The 1940 Olympics in Finland were canceled when the Soviet Union invaded Helsinki, so Robinson gave up his dream of getting a medal in the broad jump. Instead, he relaxed over the summer, enjoying some well-deserved time off after a phenomenal, but often difficult, first year at UCLA.

When Jackie returned to UCLA in the fall, something entirely unexpected happened. "I didn't think anything could come into my life that would be more vital to me than my sports career," Jackie reflected years later. "I believed that until my best friend introduced me to Rachel Isum." Jackie had been shyly watching Rachel for a couple weeks, too bashful to walk up to her and say hello. She was tall, very pretty, and had a confident style—a combination that kept Jackie staring at her, but also kept him too nervous to approach her.

Finally, Jackie's best friend ran out of patience with Jackie's shyness. "Haven't you met her yet?" he asked one afternoon as Jackie peeked at Rachel from a safe distance. "Well, come on! You'd better meet her before classes really get going and she disappears." With that, Jackie's friend dragged Jackie over to meet her. As Jackie recalled: "I didn't have the slightest idea I was meeting a young lady who would become the most important person in my life."

Rachel Annetta Isum was a seventeen-year-old nursing student who lived at home with her parents and brothers. She cared tenderly for her father, Charles, who had been injured in World War I. Like a guardian angel, Rachel had helped her father for years, even when he had fallen close to death a few times. Rachel's mother, Zellee, worked as a caterer, serving many rich white

JACKIE ROBINSON: AN AMERICAN HERO **53**

customers in Hollywood and Beverly Hills. Zellee was an elegant and stylish woman who had taught her daughter how to dress well, how to fix her hair, and, most importantly, how to be confident.

Even so, Rachel sometimes felt unattractive. She feared her cheeks were too round and her hair too thick. She was darker than her mother, and she worried about that, too. Unfortunately, as a result of the racism of that time, Rachel was ashamed of her dark skin. Later, Rachel would recall that she always noticed that Jackie wore snow-white shirts, and she could not understand why he would call attention to his very dark skin in this way. But then Rachel realized that Robinson was proud of his dark color. "He was never, ever ashamed of his color," Rachel marveled. Writer John Crosby would later describe Robinson as "the blackest black man as well as one of the handsomest I ever saw." It was this racial pride that taught Rachel to see her own dark skin as beautiful, too.

Before they were ever introduced, Rachel knew who Jackie Robinson was—she had, in fact, been watching him, too. She had seen him play football even back in high school and had thought he was conceited because of the way he always stood on the field with his hands on his hips, looking full of himself. However, when Rachel first met Jackie and saw his warm, genuine smile, she knew right away that he was anything but stuck up.

On their first date, Jackie asked Rachel to the Homecoming dance at the Los Angeles Biltmore Hotel. Rachel was lovely in a black dress and matching hat with fox trim. Jackie wore his one good suit. It was an uncomfortable evening for the young couple. Jackie did not dance well, and Rachel wondered if he even liked her. "I kept wondering on the ride home if he would kiss me," Rachel recalled. "I really wanted him to kiss me." But all she got was a quick peck on the cheek. Once again Robinson's shyness had kicked in.

Rachel and Jackie began dating and growing to like one another, but there were major differences. Rachel was dedicated to her studies. She had wanted to become a doctor, but her mother convinced her to switch to nursing. She was enrolled in the five-year Bachelor of Science nursing program at UCLA. Jackie, on the other hand, preferred sports to studying, and he thought he would someday coach high school sports.

But even with their differences, Rachel saw Jackie as a possible marriage prospect, and one day she took Jackie Robinson home to meet her parents. From the start, Rachel's father was not happy. Rachel was still his little girl, and he resented this big star athlete who was older than she was. "My father was tremendously jealous of Jack," Rachel explained. Rachel's mother, however, was thrilled by Jackie. Zellee saw Jackie as a charming, kind young man, a dream match for her daughter.

And as a result, Jackie was accepted—"[My father] sulked and rumbled . . . But my mother never budged, and my mother had the last word in our household," Rachel remembered.

When Jackie Robinson took Rachel to meet his family, she had doubts. Brother Edgar seemed mentally impaired. Brother Mack had a retarded infant son. She worried about Jackie's family. However, Rachel loved Mallie Robinson, who was kind and gracious. And Mallie immediately saw Rachel as the perfect wife for her son. Like Jackie, Rachel did not smoke or drink, and she was a studious, good girl. Rachel wisely understood that "Mallie thought of me the way my mother thought of Jack."

And the way Jackie and Rachel thought of each other made their relationship very special and precious. Jackie Robinson was seeing Rachel Isum as a future wife, and as such he was very respectful of her. Though they were falling in love with each other, both had very high standards, and intimacy would have to wait.

The 1940 UCLA football season opened with high hopes with Jackie Robinson as the superstar. But, though he played well, the season was a disappointment. Robinson was in an athletic and academic slump. His grades were going down, and he was worrying a lot about his future. When a white athlete of this time finished his college career, the professional teams would be coming to call on him. But for a young black man, these opportunities did not exist. Although Robinson was close to finishing at UCLA and getting a degree, he decided to quit and get a job.

Jackie's first job involved working as an athletic director at a National Youth Administration camp for kids. He was hired to arrange sports activities for young people from poor families. Many of these kids came from rough backgrounds, and they were more interested in getting into trouble than into sports—a fact that frustrated Jackie. But this job would not last for long.

The world was plunging into war, with armies rolling across Europe. Everybody knew it would not be long before America was involved too. So the youth camp was closed and turned into an army camp to receive new soldiers. The Selective Service System required all men between 21 and 35 to register for possible induction into the military. On December 7, 1941, Japanese planes bombed Pearl Harbor—the wait for America to join World War II was over.

Jackie's next job was a good one as a truck driver with Lockheed Aircraft in Burbank. Meanwhile, Rachel continued her nursing career. Then, her father's death in the spring brought the couple closer together. Jackie became the man in Rachel's life. While neither of them wanted to get married at once, Robinson wanted to give Rachel some sign of his commitment. He had a charm bracelet made for her featuring miniature pieces of sports equipment. Rachel was thrilled with the gift, and she wore the bracelet proudly.

Still, Rachel was determined to finish her degree—it meant more to her than love at that point in her life. "I had a sense of boundaries and goals, of tasks that had to be finished," she said. "I had seen too many good women, good students, fall into marriages after only a year or two [of college]. I couldn't be like that." And if time apart from Jack was what Rachel needed to finish college, she would soon get her wish.

On March 23, 1942, Jackie Robinson was drafted into the United States Army. He went to the National Guard Armory in Pasadena and was sent to Fort Riley, Kansas, for thirteen weeks of basic training. Fort Riley was the major training camp for the infantry scheduled to go overseas.

Jackie was rated as "excellent" after his weeks of basic training. And since he had four years of college, Robinson was qualified for Officer Candidate School (OCS). But when he first applied, he was turned down with no explanation. Instead, he was given the task of caring for the horses in the stables. He saw white men with less education and skill advance quickly. When asked why black men were not given officer training, Secretary of War Stimson said they did not have leadership qualities.

The ugliness of racism had plagued the United

States military for nearly two hundred years. Even though black men served in every American war beginning with the American Revolution, they were treated as second-class citizens. When Robinson entered the Army, segregation laws required that white officers would lead all black units. The U.S. Navy banned blacks except for kitchen duty. The Marine Corps had segregated units, and even the Red Cross refused blood plasma donated by blacks.

Robinson was not even welcome on the baseball team. Excited to see a team at Fort Riley, Jackie ran out to the field to join the practice one afternoon. Many of the white soldiers snickered when an officer said to Jackie, "You have to play with the colored team." Everyone knew that there was no "colored team"—even Jackie. He knew he was being made fun of, but he kept his temper and just turned around and walked slowly and sadly off the field.

When Jackie complained to his friend and fellow soldier, heavyweight champion Joe Louis, about being refused officer training, Louis contacted a friend in government in Washington, D.C. Finally, on November 1, Robinson was accepted into OCS. On January 28, 1943, Jackie Robinson became a 2nd lieutenant with gold bars on his uniform, and this honor meant a lot to him. When he went on leave, he visited Rachel in San Francisco, where she was doing her final years of nursing training. Robinson gave Rachel an engagement ring with a tiny diamond, and she accepted his proposal of marriage.

Back at Fort Riley, Robinson was assigned to a truck battalion and named morale officer of his company. The position of morale officer gave him the duty of listening to soldiers' complaints and trying to make changes. When some black soldiers told Robinson about bad conditions in the Post Exchange, he acted. The Post Exchange, where soldiers went to relax, was segregated, as was everything else. Blacks were confined to a few seats. Even when seats were available in the white area, the blacks could not use them. Robinson called the provost marshal to request more seats in the black area. The marshal, not realizing that Robinson was black, lowered his voice and said, "Well, let's be reasonable, Lt. Robinson. Let me put it this way: how would you like to have your wife sitting next to a nigger?" Robinson remembered his reaction: "Pure rage took over. I was shouting at the top of my voice." In the end, however, more seats were given to black soldiers.

Jackie Robinson was not punished for blowing up at the marshal, but, coincidentally or not, he was transferred to Camp Hood in Texas shortly after the phone argument. At Camp Hood, racism was very obvious. Robinson was barred from the Officers' Club. He and other black soldiers were housed in filthy tents in a muddy field, while white soldiers lived in clean brick buildings. But this was only the beginning of what would become a major incident marring Robinson's military service.

Jackie Robinson went regularly to the hospital to check on the progress of his recovery from an ankle injury he had gotten during basic training. One evening he boarded the bus to go to the hospital. He headed for the back of the bus, where black people were expected to sit. But then he saw a familiar face. Virginia Jones was the wife of a black friend, First Lt. Gordon Jones. Although she was an African-American, she was light-skinned. She called out to Robinson, and he sat down beside her in the middle of the bus. Soon they were chatting. The white bus driver turned around and demanded Robinson leave his seat and go to the rear of the bus. The bus driver probably thought Virginia Jones was a white woman, making the fact that she was having a friendly conversation with a black man all the more shocking.

Robinson later explained, "I had no intention of being intimidated into moving into the back of the bus . . . I knew what my rights were." When the bus driver yelled at him, Robinson yelled back. He pointed out that the Army did not allow segregation on military bases, and the bus was now on federal land. Robinson said he could sit wherever he wanted.

The bus driver called the military police, and they met the bus, taking Robinson into custody. He was taken to the military police guard room. The MPs later complained that Robinson was disrespectful to them and even accused Robinson, who never drank alcohol, of being drunk.

Jackie Robinson was placed under military arrest. At 1:45 on August 2nd, he faced two charges—behaving with disrespect to a superior officer and disobeying an order to remain in a room. The case was the *United States v. 2nd Lt. Jack R. Robinson.*

Jackie Robinson took the stand in his own defense. He denied being disrespectful, even though the white officers had called him a racial epithet—the n-word. Poignantly, Robinson recalled talking to his grandmother, a former slave. He said she told him he must never let any man lower him by accepting ugly words as his due. She told him to stand up and be a man because no matter what white people called him, he *was* a man. The trial lasted four hours. Robinson was found not guilty on all charges. Soon Jackie Robinson would be honorably relieved from active duty in the United States Army by reason of physical disqualification as a result of his ankle injury.

During his time in the Army, relations had become strained between Jackie Robinson and Rachel Isum. It was hard being separated from one another. At one point she even returned his engagement ring and bracelet. When Robinson returned home to Pasadena, all he could think of was seeing Rachel again, but he was too stubborn to call her. Seeing that her son was miserable and in love, Mallie Robinson told Jackie to stop being so proud and give Rachel a call. Jackie sheepishly had to admit that his mother was right—he called Rachel up, and she was warm. Robinson rushed up to San Francisco, and she put the engagement ring back on her finger.

Jackie Robinson was now twenty-six without any real prospects in life. He still had his strong faith in God, and he believed there was something important in store for him. He just had not found out what it was.

Then Jackie remembered a conversation he had had back in the Army. He had been passing a camp in Kentucky, and he saw a black man playing baseball. He found out the man belonged to the Negro National Baseball League. Though barred from playing professional baseball in the major leagues because of his color, Robinson could still play baseball in the Negro League.

Robinson wrote a letter to the owner of the Kansas City Monarchs in the Negro League. A prompt answer came. If he could make the team, the Monarchs would pay him $300 a month. Robinson asked for $400, and the team agreed. Robinson was to report for spring training in Houston, Texas.

Chapter 6

The Brave Experiment

Decades before Jackie Robinson was even born, there were, in fact, black players in major league baseball. The first black player, "Fleet" Walker, was a catcher for the Toledo (Ohio) Blue Stockings, which became a major-league team in 1884. But as harsh segregation laws were enforced in housing, transportation, and other areas, sports were also affected. The Chicago White Stockings in 1887 led a movement encouraged by racist white fans and players to ban black players completely.

In the 1920s, blacks began forming their own clubs, and the National Association of Colored Professional Baseball Clubs was created. By 1945, the Negro Leagues were thriving. In March 1945, Jackie Robinson reported to spring training. He was a member of the Kansas City Monarchs, the best team in the Negro League. Among their players was the legendary pitcher Leroy "Satchel" Paige. Up until this moment Robinson had never even seen a Negro League game.

Almost at once, Robinson noticed big

problems. For one thing, when he asked for his contract, he was told the letter he got accepting him was it. Then Robinson found out that "spring training" was not getting ready for the regular season. It *was* the regular season.

The first game was against the Chicago American Giants. Getting to the playing field meant a grueling bus trip, stays in filthy hotels with restrooms too dirty to use, and frustration for Robinson. During the game, the scoreboard displayed the wrong numbers. Still, this was all Jackie Robinson had, and he made the most of it. In 45 league games he hit ten doubles, four triples, and five home runs. But he longed with all his heart to play in the majors. A teammate later said of Jackie, "We'd ride for miles and miles on the bus, and his whole talk was, 'Well, you guys better get ready because pretty soon [major league] baseball's going to sign one of us."

Still, the managers of major league teams denied that there was a ban on black players. They said that no black player was good enough to make any team in the majors. Or they said white Southerners would not stand for it if blacks appeared on the field. There would be violence.

But there was something stirring in the world of major league baseball—something Jackie Robinson hoped for but knew nothing about. In 1943, at the headquarters of the Brooklyn Dodgers in Brooklyn Heights, the new president,

Wesley Branch Rickey, had a daring idea. What if the team could find a really outstanding black player and hire him to replace some of the white talent lost in World War II?

Branch Rickey was a character who spoke in long, flowery sentences. He shot off his mouth so often that his office was nicknamed "the cave of winds." But because he did his job so well, Rickey himself was nicknamed "The Brain." Over sixty years old now, Rickey was a devout, Bible-believing Christian. He was a great manager, having introduced the idea of training young players in farm clubs before advancing them into the major-league clubs.

Rickey hated segregation with a passion because of something that happened to him when he was the coach of the Ohio Wesleyan baseball team in 1904. The team had just one black player when they played Notre Dame that day. Afterward, the tired players headed for their hotel. All were welcome except the one black—Charles Thomas. Rickey pleaded with the hotel clerk to let Thomas share his room that night, and the clerk agreed. But Rickey never forgot Thomas's reaction. Up in the room, Rickey saw Thomas sitting with his head down, staring sadly at his hands. "It's my hands, isn't it, Mr. Rickey?" Thomas asked quietly. "If only they were white, I'd be treated as good as anybody." Seeing the young black man's humiliation and sorrow, Rickey replied that one day it wouldn't matter what color they were. From that moment, Rickey resolved that if ever in his life he got the chance to strike a blow against racial segregation, he would do it.

In addition to fighting racism, Rickey also wanted to win games. When asked why he wanted to recruit black players, Rickey plainly answered: "First, to win a pennant; I think there's some good colored players. Second reason is . . . it's right!" So Rickey sent his men around the country very quietly with this mission: find the perfect black baseball player. Find a man who could run, throw and hit with power. Equally important, Rickey told his men, find a man with character. Rickey did not want a player who would create a scandal or who was more interested in partying than in baseball.

The name of Jack Roosevelt Robinson came up shortly. Robinson was a great player. He was, like Rickey, a devout Methodist who did not smoke or drink. Though unmarried, he was engaged to a grounded, hardworking, and intelligent young woman.

Branch Rickey had his man, but now he had to make sure he could pull this brave experiment off. He brought up the idea with his friends at a card game. They did not support him. They thought bringing in a black player would be a disaster. Rickey's wife and son feared a firestorm of protest that would ruin Branch Rickey and sink the Dodgers. Branch Rickey barely got any encouragement at all. He went ahead with his plan anyway.

The plan was to send a Dodger scout to bring Jackie Robinson to his office on a phony story. Supposedly Rickey wanted to start a new club, the Brown Dodgers, to give black men the chance to play baseball. It would be nice, but it would not be the majors.

Jackie Robinson was sick of the Negro League by this time. He planned to quit and get a job as a high-school coach in Los Angeles. He would marry Rachel Isum and forever bury his dream of playing baseball for a living. And in June 1945, Rachel graduated from the nursing program with honors, receiving the Florence Nightingale Award as the best clinical nurse in her class. It looked to Jackie as though his life was all mapped out.

But on August 24th, a stranger walked up to Jackie Robinson after a Negro League game. The white man, whose name was Clyde Sukeforth, said he was representing Branch Rickey of the Brooklyn Dodgers. As he talked about the Brown Dodgers, Robinson listened with interest.

On August 28th, Jackie Robinson arrived at 215 Montague Street in Brooklyn. Rickey, an older white man with bushy eyebrows, sat behind a huge desk. "He had a way of cutting through red tape and getting down to basics," Jackie later said of Rickey. After the two men stared at each other for a minute, Rickey's first question was, "You got a girl?" When Jackie replied that he did, Rickey said, "When we get through today, you may want to call her up, because there are times when a man needs a woman by his side."

Jackie's heart pounded. He began to suspect he had not been brought to Brooklyn to discuss playing for the Brown Dodgers. Then, Rickey revealed his brave experiment—Robinson was under serious consideration to play for the Brooklyn Dodgers' farm team, the Montreal Royals, and then join the Brooklyn Dodgers itself. Jackie Robinson later recalled being "thrilled, scared and excited," as well as "speechless." Rickey asked Robinson if he thought he could play for the Dodgers, and Robinson said yes. But then came the hard part—what could have been the heartbreaking deal-ender.

Rickey told Robinson that times ahead would be tough. Robinson would be verbally abused and threatened. It would be worse than anything he had ever seen before. "I know you're a good ballplayer—but this is something beyond," Rickey said. "I've got to know if you've got the guts."

"Do you want a player who doesn't have the guts to fight back?" Robinson asked.

"I'm looking for a ballplayer," Rickey said, "with the guts *not* to fight back."

Before Jackie Robinson could give his answer, Rickey came out from behind his chair and dramatized the situations Robinson would face. Rickey acted out the role of a rude hotel clerk refusing accommodations, a white waiter refusing to serve him, a foul-mouthed teammate attacking his parents, beanballs, spikings, curses. Rickey even jabbed a fist at Robinson's head. "His acting was so convincing," Robinson later wrote, "that I found myself chain-gripping my fingers behind my back!"

Robinson was deeply moved by Rickey's passion. He had no doubt of Rickey's sincerity. Robinson finally said he would agree to the conditions—for Rachel Isum, who would be his wife; for his mother; for all the black youngsters who would come after him; for himself—and finally, he admitted, "I had already begun to feel I had to do it for Branch Rickey." Branch Rickey then handed Robinson a copy of *A Life of Christ*. He pointed to the words about turning the other cheek when struck. Robinson nodded. He understood.

The brave experiment had begun.

Jackie Robinson reached the street outside with a contract in his pocket. His signing bonus was $3500. His salary would be $600 a month. But he had to keep it all a secret until Branch Rickey made the fateful announcement himself.

Jackie Robinson kept the secret, telling Rachel and his family only that something wonderful had happened. On October 23, Branch

Rickey made the signing of Jackie Robinson public. There was both support and opposition, but nobody knew what would happen when Robinson took the field.

Jackie Robinson and Rachel Isum planned their wedding with Rachel's mother in full control. Zellee Isum had been married twice, but had never had a real ceremony, so she made up for that with her own daughter's wedding. On a Sunday afternoon, February 10, Jackie and Rachel were married. The church was jammed with family and friends. Then the newlyweds were off to the Clark Hotel in Los Angeles. The day had had a few mishaps, like misplaced rings and missing flowers, but it never bothered Rachel: "I felt that all my troubles had melted away, and that a wonderful new life was beginning for Jack and for me."

On February 28, 1945, Rachel and Jackie Robinson were ready to board an American Airlines plane for Daytona Beach and spring training. Jackie's mother, Mallie, handed her son a shoebox containing hard-boiled eggs and fried chicken—just in case something went wrong and they needed to grab a bite.

But Mallie Robinson and the two newlyweds had no idea just how much would go wrong over the next few days.

The Robinsons were glad they were flying, not riding a segregated bus or train, to Daytona Beach.

And both Jackie and Rachel dressed up for the trip, particularly Rachel in her ermine coat. "I thought when I wore it," Rachel explained, "everyone would know I belonged on that plane . . . or wherever I happened to be."

But during their trip, neither Rachel nor Jackie were treated like they belonged. They flew overnight and arrived in New Orleans at sunrise, but then they were bumped from the next flight to Daytona so that white people could have their seats. In the meantime, they went to a coffee shop at the airport for something to eat, but they were turned away. Then they were sent to a filthy hotel, the only one where blacks were allowed. It was crawling with cockroaches and water bugs. Robinson had seen many such hotels when he played with the Negro League, but for Rachel it was a nasty shock. The Robinsons could not lie down on the dirty bed, so they sat up in chairs all night, covered with newspapers.

Finally, there was another flight, but the Robinsons were again bumped for white passengers. Jackie gave up on flying, and they took a bus for Daytona. It was a sixteen-hour ride to Jacksonville, another sixteen hours to Daytona Beach. The Robinsons found seats that reclined, and they were getting some sleep when the bus driver roused them in the middle of the night. Even though they were sitting in the black section, some white passengers wanted their seats, so would they please move farther back? The back seats did not recline, so there was no more sleep. Rachel buried her head in the seat in front of her and cried all night.

Finally, on March 4, Jackie Robinson put on his gray Montreal Royals baseball uniform and walked into the clubhouse for the first time. Branch Rickey had warned all the players that they had to be gentlemen, no matter how they felt about blacks. But Robinson was nervous. He glanced out at the green field to see two hundred players running, fielding and throwing the ball. They were talking, laughing together. They were all white. "And it seemed that every one of those men stopped suddenly in his tracks and that four hundred eyes were trained on me," Jackie remembered.

Next, reporters crowded around Jackie and one other black player, focusing on Robinson. "How do you think you'll get along with these white boys?" they asked.

"I've gotten along with white boys in high school, Pasadena, UCLA and the Army. I don't see why these should be any different," Jackie responded calmly.

"But what if a white pitcher throws at your head?" the reporters asked, determined to upset Jackie.

"I'll duck," Jackie answered with a smile.

On March 17, there was a game between the Montreal Royals and the Brooklyn Dodgers.

Robinson would have to show he deserved to play alongside the seasoned Dodger players. It was Sunday, and four thousand fans came, including a thousand blacks who were well aware that history was being made right before their very eyes. The blacks were forced to sit in a small segregated section, but there were so many eager black fans that they spilled over onto the grounds. When Robinson took the field, he heard a few faint boos and a lot of cheering. He was under a great deal of pressure, and he played flawlessly at second base, but failed to get a hit.

A scheduled game between Montreal and the Jersey City Giants was set for Jacksonville. Although Jacksonville's population was about fifty percent black, the city asked that the two black players not show up since it was against the city's laws for black and white men to play sports together. Branch Rickey told city officials that if *all* his team was not welcome, none of his team would play. Rickey said that if the price of keeping his black players in the lineup was missing an exhibition game in the South, then so be it. Angry that Rickey would not back down, the city of Jacksonville voted to cancel the game.

But the racial insults were not reserved just for games played in the South. In New Jersey, the Newark Bears' outfielder refused to play in the game if Robinson was allowed on the field. And in Syracuse, New York, a player shoved a black cat in

Robinson's direction as Jackie walked out to take his turn at bat. "Hey Jackie, there's your cousin," the player shouted as his teammates laughed loudly. Jackie's response was to hit a double down the left-field line. When the next player hit a single, Jackie scored, yelling, "I guess my cousin's pretty happy now," as he ran by the Syracuse dugout.

Branch Rickey had been warned that there would be rioting and bloodshed in Baltimore if Robinson walked out on the field. At the first game of the Baltimore series, on a bitterly cold night, only 3,415 fans showed up. Rachel Robinson was sitting in the stands when her husband came out. The man behind her snarled, "Let's give it to him now." Racial insults swirled through the stands like confetti. Rachel Robinson was frightened for Jackie's safety, but in spite of the loud torrent of abuse, there was none of the predicted violence.

The next day, the team arrived for a double-header. This time, 25,000 fans filled the stadium, including 10,000 blacks. The white fans again booed loudly when Robinson took the field. The next night, they played again in Baltimore, and Robinson got three hits and scored four runs to lead the Royals to a 10–0 victory. Jackie Robinson felt a whole lot better. He had survived the pressure of opening day in New Jersey and the hatred of Baltimore's white fans. He was still standing and doing it proudly. Branch Rickey knew what Jackie had been going through. As a result, Rickey sat in the front row, cheering Robinson at every exhibition game.

When spring training ended, Jackie Robinson returned to Montreal. He and Rachel basked in the much friendlier atmosphere of the Canadian city, where racism was rarely experienced. Rachel went apartment hunting, steeling herself for possible rejection, but the French Canadians welcomed her, treating her no differently than a white woman. Soon she had rented a nice apartment. When the Robinsons moved in, a large group of neighbors came to visit and offer help. The children offered to help the now pregnant Rachel Robinson with the move. Both Jackie and Rachel enjoyed all this kindness, especially after some of their experiences in the American South over the past months.

When the regular season started, Jackie Robinson continued to get a mixed reception, depending on the city the Royals played in. But in Baltimore there was always the threat of serious violence. One night, an angry mob of Baltimore fans surrounded the clubhouse after a game. They chanted and shouted, "Come out of there, Robinson . . . we know you're in there! We're gonna get you!" Robinson was trapped by the mob until 1 a.m., when the fans finally left. Thankfully, three of Robinson's teammates stayed with him and made sure he got to the hotel safely.

"Hey, you oughta be behind a pack of mules, black boy—not playing baseball!" an angry

Baltimore fan screamed at the next game.

"You let one of 'em in and pretty soon you all will be out of a job!" Even the Orioles' manager shouted taunts at the Montreal players and racist garbage at Jackie. But, though the Baltimore fans screamed their hatred for Robinson, they came to see him in larger numbers than ever before in stadium history. He was the big draw. Everybody wanted to see this man they had heard so much about. So, in spite of the abuse heaped on the head of Jackie Robinson in Baltimore, he was making money for the city, and Baltimore loved it.

While putting up with abuse from other teams' fans was rough, dealing with other players was becoming Robinson's most daunting challenge. Bill Nack wrote in *Sports Illustrated*, "Robinson was the target of racial epithets and flying cleats . . . of pitchers throwing at his head and legs and catchers spitting on his shoes."

Even Robinson's own teammates did not welcome him with open arms, but gradually he was winning them over. Robinson was very sensitive about pushing himself on them. He did not sit with anyone else at lunch unless he was invited. Little by little, he got more invitations to join his teammates at the lunch tables and for card games.

Robinson was enduring all the abuse with dignity, just as he promised Rickey he would, but it was affecting his health. He couldn't sleep or eat, and he was nauseated frequently. A doctor warned

Jackie that he was close to a nervous breakdown and told him to take some time off. Jackie agreed— for exactly twenty-four hours. "Doctor's orders or not, I just couldn't keep my mind off baseball," Jackie explained. "I just had to go back."

On the field, Robinson was doing very well. He led the league in hitting with a .349 average. He finished second in stolen bases and drove in 66 runs. The Montreal Royals won the International League pennant by nineteen and a half games. In the playoffs, they defeated the Newark Bears and Syracuse Chiefs to become league champions. The final test was for the champion of the International League to face the American Association. In 1946, the American Association champion was the Louisville Colonels. So Robinson and the Royals headed to Louisville, Kentucky for the first game.

When news spread that Robinson would be playing in Louisville, black fans flocked to buy tickets. But there were only 466 seats for black fans. The black people found a way. There were plenty of white seats available, so they paid white owners of the choice seats high prices and got them. Others who could not afford to do this watched the game from strategic vantage points. One fan climbed a telephone pole. Three hundred more fans clung to the roof of an old house, while others stood on top of tool sheds or climbed onto the freight trains at the nearby tracks.

When Robinson came onto the field, he was

met by boos and catcalls. The white fans screamed insults, shouting names like "watermelon eater," "chicken thief," and the more familiar epithets. "I'd been insulted by the experts," Jackie said after the game, "but never like this." The game was delayed, and the boos grew louder. Robinson endured it stoically, but his game suffered. The Royals lost the game. They lost the next day too, but won the third game. Now, lagging behind Louisville, 2–1, they headed for Montreal.

Never before had the Montreal fans cheered so loudly for their team or booed so angrily at a visiting team. The Louisville Colonels got a taste of their own medicine as Robinson led the Royals to victory in the fourth game by hitting a game-winning single in the tenth inning. In the fifth and final game, Robinson got three hits and led his team to victory in front of nearly 20,000 screaming fans. The Royals were crowned Little World Series champions for defeating the American Association team.

Montreal fans ran for the clubhouse to honor their hero—Jackie Robinson. They surrounded Robinson, hugging and kissing him. They lifted him to their shoulders, and tears filled his eyes. The celebration was heartfelt and wonderful, but Robinson wanted to go home and rest. Happy fans chased him for thee blocks as he hurried toward home. A friend observed, "It was probably the only day in history that a black man ran from a white mob with love instead of lynching on its mind."

On November 18, 1946, Jackie Robinson, Jr. was born at Good Samaritan Hospital in Los Angeles.

When spring training began in 1947 in Havana, Cuba, Jackie Robinson knew that being called up to play for the Brooklyn Dodgers depended on how well he did in a series of games between the Montreal Royals and the Brooklyn Dodgers.

In the seven-game series between the Dodgers and Royals, Robinson batted an incredible .625 and stole seven bases. On April 10, Branch Rickey decided he had seen enough. His brave experiment had given him the proof he needed. On the morning of April 9, 1947, reporters jammed into the press box at a Royals exhibition game. But this time it was not to needle Jackie Robinson about how he'd handle playing with white players or what he'd do if a pitcher threw a ball at his head. This time it was to receive a one-line announcement:

"Brooklyn announces the purchase of the contract of Jack Roosevelt Robinson from Montreal. Signed, Branch Rickey."

Chapter 7

Grace Under Pressure

"Whenever I hear my wife read fairy tales to my little boy, I'll listen. I know now that dreams do come true." Jackie Robinson wrote these words a few days after first entering the Brooklyn Dodgers' clubhouse in 1947. Perhaps there were no available lockers, and Jackie had to hang his clothes on a nail. Perhaps his teammates were none too friendly. But when Jackie was handed a white uniform with a blue number 42 on the back, his dream was coming true.

On April 15, 1947, the Brooklyn Dodgers opened their regular season in Ebbets Field against the Boston Braves. An overflow crowd packed the stadium, eager to see Robinson play. Rachel Robinson, who described herself as "very, very excited and very, very nervous," sat with their baby son in her arms. Jackie scanned the crowd and finally spotted his wife and son and smiled in spite of his own nervousness.

Robinson's first game was, as one reporter described it, "uneventful." "I did a miserable job," Jackie honestly admitted. But three days later, the Dodgers played the New York Giants, and Robinson smacked his first major league home run. Then, on the following weekend, the biggest ever Saturday afternoon crowd in National League history, 52,000 people, crowded the Giants' ballpark. Robinson got three hits in four at-bats, and even though the Dodgers lost that game, things were looking up for Jackie. But then, on April 22, just before heading to Philadelphia, a period of crushing pressure began.

The sight of a black man in a Dodger uniform stirred up great hatred among the Phillies' players and fans. "Next time you take the field," Robinson was warned in an anonymous letter, "I'll kill you." Another letter said, "Get out of baseball or else." The Phillies' manager, Ben Chapman, contacted Branch Rickey, telling him to keep Robinson at home because his players would not come if he was there. Rickey responded, saying that was fine. The Phillies could just forfeit the games, and the Dodgers would win without even having to play. The Phillies backed down, but tensions were rising.

Alabaman Ben Chapman had a reputation for making life miserable for rookies on the opposing team. Now that there was a black rookie, Chapman encouraged his team to attack Robinson viciously. As Robinson appeared, Chapman and several of the Phillies players cut loose with a volley of ugly taunts, all focusing on Robinson's race. They mocked his full lips, his hair, even his moral character. They yelled for him to return to the cotton fields or the jungles. The abuse continued throughout the series with Philadelphia. Jackie remembered how Branch Rickey had acted out the name-calling and abuse Jackie would have to face. Rickey had not exaggerated.

At one point, the Phillies sat in the dugout pointing their bats at Robinson and making machine-gun-like noises. Robinson sat quietly, pretending, as always, that it didn't bother him. But beneath his cool exterior, Jackie was near his breaking point. "For one wild and rage-crazed minute, I thought, 'To hell with Mr. Rickey's noble experiment,'" Jackie remembered. "I thought what a glorious, cleansing thing it would be to let go . . . to stride over to that Phillies dugout, grab one of those [players], and smash his teeth in."

But then something happened that began to make Jackie feel better. Until this game against the Phillies, many of Jackie's teammates had been unfriendly. One particular player, Ed Stanky, had been downright cruel. "I want you to know," Ed had told Jackie, "that I don't like you being on this team. And I want you to know that I don't like you." But Stanky had had enough of the Phillies' taunts. Suddenly, he realized the unbearable humiliation that Jackie was bravely enduring. Stanky turned to the Phillies dugout and screamed, "Listen, you yellow-bellied cowards! Why don't you yell at somebody who can answer back?" It was a turning point, and Jackie knew it.

And, certainly, not all of Jackie's experiences with fans and other teams were bad. Far from it. In Brooklyn, whites and blacks alike flocked to Ebbets Field to see this celebrity. Tickets went like ice cream in August. Most of the white fans were on Robinson's side, and they favored the integration of baseball. After the games, the fans stood in long lines for Robinson's autograph. Robinson was getting many whites to re-examine their attitude on race—and at the same time, he was filling blacks with pride.

When Robinson played his first game as a major leaguer in Chicago at Wrigley Field, thousands of black fans traveled long distances by train and car just to get a glimpse of their new hero. They were not dressed casually, as the white fans were. They wore their Sunday best, white shirts and suits, shined shoes and straw hats. When Robinson was at bat, there was rumbling applause. When he missed, deep groans. A week after that game, Robinson received a letter from an elderly black woman who lived in a small, poor town in Arkansas. She had sat close to her radio and listened to the game. "There is no greater thrill than a broadcast of a Dodgers' ballgame," she wrote. "We are so very proud of you."

Jackie Robinson was an intensely competitive player who inspired his teammates and intimidated his opponents. The sports world began to concoct nicknames for him. He was "the black meteor," an "ebony Ty Cobb," and, based on the way he sprinted and danced on the field to confuse the other team, "the Bojangles of baseball." In the first ten games of May, he hit a blazing .395.

Racial incidents continued to mar the 1947 season, however. A Cincinnati pitcher spewed racial insults at Robinson. A Chicago player deliberately kicked him. Robinson started to retaliate against the kicker, but then he stopped himself, once again remembering his promise to Rickey. By the time the 1947 season was half over, pitchers had hit Robinson seven times, more than anyone else in the National League in the entire preceding season. He was the league's most popular target.

Robinson's closest friend on the team was Pee Wee Reese, a slick-fielding shortstop from Kentucky. Most people thought that a Southerner would be the last person to befriend Jackie. Even Reese's own parents were baffled by their son's behavior. But Pee Wee explained it simply: "I put myself in Robinson's place. I said to myself, suppose Negroes were in the majority in this country, and for years baseball had been closed to white players." Reese understood how Jackie felt. And sometimes when the crowd's taunts and name-calling got to be too much, Reese would walk over and put an arm around his friend's shoulder. More than once, that display of kindness silenced the crowd.

Before long, Robinson had a new problem. He had become very famous. Like a movie star, he was chased by well-wishers and autograph hounds wherever he went. A national poll in 1947 showed Jackie Robinson to be the second most popular man in America, outpolled only by the singer Bing Crosby. He received so much fan mail that the Dodgers had to hire a secretary to handle it. Robinson signed each response.

But even with all his fame, on the Dodger road trips he was just another black man who had to settle for dirty hotel rooms and poor restaurants. And despite his great performances on the playing field and his growing fame, Jackie Robinson was paid only $5,000, the minimum for a major-leaguer. He and his wife and son lived in a one-room apartment that didn't even have a kitchen. But then Branch Rickey lifted the ban on players endorsing products, and Robinson began to pick up more money promoting commercial products in black newspapers. On September 23, 1947, a Jackie Robinson Day was held at Ebbets Field, and the Robinsons received gifts worth $10,000, including a Cadillac, a television set, and a chest of silver. Robinson also made a theatrical tour, which brought in $2,500. He became a popular radio guest, and he was contacted about writing a book and appearing in a movie on his own life. Finally, the Robinsons were able to move to a tenement in Brooklyn, where they had a kitchen and more room. Things were beginning to look up.

On the baseball field, Jackie Robinson was trying to lead the Dodgers to a National League pennant. The Dodgers had won the pennant in 1916 and 1920. Then followed many lean years when they fielded very poor teams. Even their most loyal fans spoke of them as "dem bums." It wasn't until 1941 that they won the pennant again. They were hungry for another in 1947. They were in first place in July but then slipped behind the Cardinals.

On August 18, 1947, the Dodgers and Cardinals met for a crucial game. Cardinal outfielder Joe Medwick spiked Robinson on the left foot, leaving a bloody wound. Later, Robinson was spiked again, slashing his left leg and knocking him down. The Cardinals were told to cease all attacks against Robinson or face grave consequences. The Dodgers and Cardinals split the series, but then the Brooklyn Dodgers surged ahead. They won the 1947 pennant, much to the fans' excitement. Jackie received a hero's welcome when he returned home. Rushing to a phone booth to call his wife, Jackie was quickly surrounded by adoring fans who, pushing and shoving to get a look at the star, trapped him inside the booth. Jackie could do nothing but smile politely at the crush of fans until a police officer broke up the crowd.

Jackie Robinson was named Rookie of the Year. He played in 151 of 154 games. He hit 12 home runs, stole a league-leading 29 bases, and batted .297. He had proved wrong all the critics who believed that a black athlete couldn't possibly compete in the major leagues. In October, the Dodgers met the New York Yankees in the World Series, where Robinson played well but not brilliantly. "We were up against the spectacular New York Yankees," Jackie said. "We fought hard, but the Yankees were a great baseball club." And even though the Dodgers lost the series, they were extremely happy with their 1947 season.

In 1948, the Dodger season opened at the Polo Grounds against the New York Giants. Robinson was in a slump until June, when he hit a grand slam home run in the first game of a doubleheader against Pittsburgh. In the second game he had three more hits, and his batting average rose to .306. He also stole his first base of the season. Although Robinson regained his stride in the second half of the season and led the Dodgers with a .296 batting average, it was not enough to keep the pennant from the Boston Braves. Robinson vowed to help his team regain the pennant in 1949.

Jackie Robinson's salary rose to $17,500 for the 1949 season, but it was still well below the league's highest salary. On April 19, 1949, Robinson hit a home run and two singles against the Giants. In June he had a .344 average, second in the league, and he led the league in runs batted in. Jackie Robinson was chosen to play in baseball's All-Star Game in July at Ebbets Field. He was having a great year when something he did not expect happened. He was asked to come to Washington to speak before the House Committee on Un-American Activities. Hearings were underway on the topic of black Americans and how loyal they were to the United States.

Jackie Robinson was perplexed. He was a thirty-year-old baseball player, an Army veteran, and someone who knew very little about politics and even less about this Washington committee. The whole problem began with some statements made by Paul Robeson, a famous black baritone and civil rights advocate. Robeson, like Jackie, had long experienced cruel and unfair treatment simply because of his skin color. It made no difference that he was a talented singer and a lawyer with a degree from Rutgers. Jackie understood Robeson's anger, and he agreed with much of what Robeson said.

But Robeson also said that American blacks were so disgusted by how they'd been treated that if they were called upon to defend their country in another war, they probably would not go. (Robeson was wrong because in the Korean War, before schools were even desegregated, 3,100 blacks died fighting for their country; and in Vietnam, while the civil rights struggle was still going on, 5,681 died in combat.)

"I was black and [Robeson] wasn't speaking for me," Robinson explained. "I had served in the Armed Forces . . . I couldn't defend my country for the racial injustices I had suffered . . . [but] I was still proud to have been in uniform." So Jackie went to Washington and said just that. Jackie was praised for his words, receiving awards from many veterans' organizations. Even so, Jackie had mixed feelings about disagreeing publicly with Robeson: "I believe he was sincerely trying to help his people."

After the All-Star Game, Robinson continued to play very well. *Time* magazine hailed him as "the ballplayer of the year." By the end of the season, his batting average was .342, and he had led the National League in stolen bases with 37. He was voted Most Valuable Player for 1949 in the National League. With his help, the Brooklyn Dodgers again won the National League pennant for 1949. In the World Series they lost again to the New York Yankees, four games to one. The Dodger fans would once again have to "wait till next year."

The incredible fame that had come to Jackie in only a few short years was always a double-edged sword. Jackie was, after all, a rather private person who was not interested in the glamor of fame. When the Robinsons bought a house, complete strangers would often knock on the door demanding that Rachel pose for pictures. If Rachel refused, the strangers became angry. "The public both idolizes and abuses celebrities and their families," Jackie once commented. And after Jackie starred in a popular movie about his own life, *The Jackie Robinson Story*, he and his family could not even go out for a simple dinner without getting mobbed.

But Jackie's fame also gave him opportunities to help young people and the poor. He worked with the Harlem YMCA, and he often visited the sick. This kind of work, along with the strong faith that his mother had instilled in him, helped keep Jackie grounded.

When the 1950 baseball season opened, Jackie Robinson was now making $35,000 a year—quite a good salary in 1950. And that extra income would come in handy; Rachel had given birth to a daughter, Sharon, on January 13. The Dodgers were confident about winning the pennant again. This time they wanted to win the World Series as well. The Brooklyn Dodgers had never won the World Series. In May, the Dodgers led the pack, but on the last day of the season, they were battling the Phillies for the pennant. It was a bitter pill indeed when the Philadelphia Phillies won. The season was a disappointment for the Dodgers and for Robinson. Though he batted an excellent .328, it wasn't enough to lift his team to victory. Then Branch Rickey left the club, to be replaced by Walter O'Malley. Robinson was sorry to see his old friend go, but their friendship remained strong until Rickey's death in 1965.

At the start of the 1951 season, Jackie found two FBI agents waiting for him at his hotel room in Cincinnati. The agents explained that the police, the Cincinnati newspaper, and the Cincinnati Reds team had all received the same frightening letter. The letter, signed simply by "Three Travelers," claimed that someone with a rifle would be hiding in a building across from the Reds' field. They would be aiming for Jackie Robinson. Jackie shrugged it off and said he wasn't worried. And Jackie's friend, Pee Wee Reese offered a joking solution: "I think we should all wear number 42. Then they will have a shooting gallery." The game went on. But at one point, Pee Wee told Robinson not to stand too close to him. "You mind moving over a little, Jack?" he joked. "This guy might be a bad shot."

In the last crucial game of the 1951 season, Jackie Robinson hit a towering home run to move the Dodgers into a tie for first place with the New York Giants. But in the three-game playoffs, the

Giants defeated the Dodgers on the strength of Giant Bobby Thomson's dramatic home run. Once again, the Dodgers were extremely disappointed. Robinson had batted an outstanding .338 with 19 home runs and 88 runs batted in that season. Even so, all of his achievements were clouded by the final loss to the Giants.

And so, the Brooklyn Dodgers began the 1952 season with very little confidence. They had suffered too much disappointment to expect a pennant this year. Jackie, however, did not lose faith, leading the Dodgers at the end of June in hitting. His batting average was .327 with 5 home runs and 11 stolen bases. And, in spite of his team's low confidence, Jackie led the Brooklyn Dodgers to another pennant. But when they faced again their old nemesis, the New York Yankees, and for the third time failed to win the World Series, Jackie felt great disappointment.

Barely five years earlier, Jackie had believed that dreams do come true. But now, an increasingly discouraged Jackie Robinson seemed to be waking up from the dream. His third child, David, had just been born. As a father of three, Jackie wondered if he should begin to pursue a different career. Was the dream over? Should he quit baseball?

Chapter 8

Champions at Sundown

"If we don't win it this time, we'll never win it." Jackie Robinson was speaking to the press in October, 1953. The Dodgers were headed once again to a World Series against the Yankees. "We have the power . . . the kind of team it takes to beat the Yankees." In spite of his worries at the end of the '52 season, Jackie had had a great year. The thirty-three-year-old's salary was bumped to $42,000, the highest in the club. Robinson played in 136 games and lifted his average to .329 with 12 home runs, 17 stolen bases, and 95 runs batted in.

But again, the Dodgers were denied. With Mickey Mantle and Billy Martin hitting homers and grand slams, the Yankees won the series in six games. Although the Dodgers had power, it was still not enough to beat their greatest rival.

As Jackie's devotion to baseball began to falter, he was developing an interest in the political world. He had been at a Washington dinner honoring the work of the Anti-Defamation League, a

Jewish organization fighting prejudice. Suddenly, President Dwight D. Eisenhower crossed the room to shake Robinson's hand. He was very moved by this gesture from the president. Robinson also met Vice-President Richard Nixon. Both Robinson and Nixon had grown up in southern California, and they had a lot of memories to exchange. But when Nixon recalled a UCLA football game and a specific play that Jackie had helped with, Jackie was amazed. Although the Robinsons had always been Democrats, Jackie's experiences with both Eisenhower and Nixon drew him to the Republican Party.

In 1953, Jackie Robinson's interest in the civil rights struggle also grew. In particular, Jackie's heart went out to young black people. "I'm grateful for all the breaks and honors and opportunities I've had," Jackie once said, "but I always believe I won't have it made until the humblest black kid in the most remote backwoods of America has it made." In an attempt to make a difference, Jackie spoke to thousands of young people about racial tolerance, moral principles, education, and family life.

The 1954 baseball season was bad for the Dodgers and for Jackie Robinson. Robinson vowed to win the pennant, as well as the National League batting title and the Most Valuable Player award again. In the month of April, he hit .368. Then he went into a bad slump, unable to get hits and rarely stealing bases anymore.

To make matters worse, Robinson's image took a downhill turn after two incidents. First, after a bitter verbal exchange with an opposing team, a frustrated Robinson tossed his bat forward, away from the dugout. The bat landed in the stands, striking, but not injuring, a female fan. Robinson's reputation for staying cool in times of stress was damaged. Next, Robinson's teammate knocked down a Braves player, and in retaliation, the Braves pitcher decked Robinson with a pitch. It was the 66th time Robinson had been hit by a pitch in the major leagues. When Robinson complained, sports writers said he was being too sensitive, too quick to see racism everywhere. Even O'Malley, who had replaced Branch Rickey, accused Jackie of whining and being too soft.

The Dodgers lost the pennant in 1954 to the Giants. Robinson had batted over .300, but he had knocked in only 59 runs, 36 fewer than he had the year before. He had stolen only 7 bases, compared to 17 in 1953 and 24 in 1952. Robinson was thirty-five, and his feet hurt almost all the time. He was weary, and he thought a lot more about quitting baseball. But he could not. The family had bought a beautiful new home in Connecticut, and Robinson's expenses were greater than they had ever been before. He needed his baseball salary.

In the fall of 1954, Jackie Robinson relaxed

and got as much rest as he could, hoping to face the next season with more strength. He enjoyed his family, Rachel, eight-year-old Jackie Jr., four-year-old Sharon, and two-year-old David. He traveled a bit, giving inspirational speeches, but mostly he took some time off.

Of the first twenty-five games of the '55 season, Brooklyn won twenty-two. One month into the season, the Dodgers led the National League by ten games. But Robinson's average was sinking. Over the summer he had gained 25 pounds, and now his body was beginning to refuse to do what he asked of it. Ankle and knee problems hounded him. Though he was not even 40, years of stress had turned his hair gray. When his batting average dropped to .244, he asked that he be benched.

"He's an old, gray fat man," one sportswriter said of Jackie as the '55 season wore on. But near the end of the season, Jackie's magic returned briefly. First, he helped Brooklyn clinch the pennant. And then the World Series against the New York Yankees loomed yet again. The Dodgers fought the defeatist fear that it would be history repeating itself once more. Jackie knew that this might be his last chance to help his team to the championship.

In the first game of the series, Robinson showed his old spark. Hitting a grounder to left field, he put everything he had into a burst of speed that took him to second base. When the next batter advanced Robinson to third, Jackie began eyeing home. From the Yankees dugout, players began shouting, "Don't worry about Robinson! He's too slow and fat!" The pitcher agreed and ignored Jackie. Big mistake. In a flash, Jackie stole home for the eighteenth time in his career. "How's that for an old, gray fat man?" he bellowed toward the Yankees dugout with a grin.

Eventually, the series was tied up at 3–3. The Dodgers got ready for the seventh and deciding game of the 1955 World Series. With a 2–0 victory, the Dodgers finally triumphed over the Yankees, claiming the World Series title for the first time in their history. Although Robinson did not play the final game of the series, the press suddenly loved Jackie again, giving him the credit for inspiring the Dodgers to victory. One sports columnist wrote, "He showed his teammates, he showed his opponents, he showed a nation—that the Dodgers *can* beat the Yankees."

But Jackie was not sure if he would return for the next season. He still wanted to play, and he hoped that winning the World Series would inspire the Dodgers to give him another season. But he continued to wonder if he should be moving in other directions.

And by this time, the brave experiment he and Branch Rickey had launched years ago had proven a great success. More than 40 black players were part of MLB teams, including Larry Doby of the Cleveland Indians, Roy Campanella of the Dodgers, the legendary Willie Mays playing for the New York Giants, Ernie Banks of the Chicago Cubs, and Henry "Hank" Aaron of the Milwaukee Braves. A black face was no longer an oddity in baseball's majors, and Jackie Robinson had opened the door for them all.

But even with his doubts about continuing playing, Robinson reported to the 1956 training camp. He had told Rachel that he had made the decision to play as long as his legs and body allowed him to. He was worried about making the team and getting on the roster, but his hard work and dedication paid off—he would be a Dodger for another season.

Not only was Jackie wearing down physically; he was also wearing down mentally. When a Milwaukee Braves player hurled a racial insult at Robinson, he responded with uncharacteristic rage. He fired a ball at the player's head, barely missing him. Robinson was seen shaking with rage as the ball crashed into a wall, then careened into the field. Robinson had endured so much abuse in silence; he finally had reached a breaking point.

In August, thirty-seven-year-old Robinson proved he was down but not yet out. He hit a two-run homer and a game-winning single against Milwaukee. On the last day of the season, the

Brooklyn Dodgers won another pennant. In the World Series, Robinson played in all seven games, and hit .250 with one home run and one game-winning hit. But in the seventh game, the Yankees defeated the Dodgers 9–0 to win the Series.

Even with an aching body, Jackie believed he had one more season in him—he still had the desire to play the game; and, perhaps more importantly, he needed dependable earnings. He now had three young children and a wife to support. Jackie Robinson had dabbled in several business ventures, including owning a clothing store, as he planned for his post-baseball life, but nothing succeeded. What Jackie really wanted to do was coach baseball, and with his talent and history, his coaching would have been a dream asset to any team. But once again, because of his skin color, it was an impossible dream at that time.

In 1956, the NAACP awarded Jackie Robinson the Spingarn Medal, given annually to a black American whose achievement brought great credit to his race. Right after receiving the Spingarn Medal, Robinson got some very good news. William H. Black, the president of a popular coffee shop chain, Chock Full o' Nuts, made a job offer. He wanted Robinson as Director of Personnel for the whole operation. Robinson was excited at the thought of dealing with the welfare of over a thousand employees, many of them black. Black had read about Robinson, and he was sure he was the man for the job. Robinson would be paid $30,000 a year, and he would have the use of a company car as well as receive stock options. Black offered a two-year contract, but he made it clear he expected Robinson to remain with the company as long as he wanted.

Then, without any warning, the Dodgers called Robinson to let him know that he had been traded to the New York Giants. Robinson was shocked, as were thousands of Dodgers fans. The idea of him playing for the Giants, bitter rivals of the Dodgers, struck him as an insult. Even so, the Giants offered Jackie a salary of $60,000, giving him second thoughts. The press then descended in a frenzy of speculation, claiming that Robinson's supposed deal with Chock Full o' Nuts was nothing more than a bargaining tool to get more money out of the Giants. Jackie was furious. Immediately, he accepted the job with Chock Full o' Nuts. "I wouldn't give them [the press] a chance to say 'I told you so.' And my baseball career was over . . . I had outsmarted baseball before baseball had outsmarted me."

Finally, Jackie Robinson was coming home. Rachel Robinson and the children would now have their husband and father home twelve months of the year. Until now, the family had to surrender Jackie to baseball between March and October every year. Jackie Robinson looked forward to his new way of life. He said that when he played baseball, he came home every October feeling like a stranger in his own family. Now he could eat dinner with his family every day and say goodnight to his children every night.

Although the big house in Connecticut had been Rachel's idea, and keeping up the expenses worried Jackie, he had grown to love the place too. He enjoyed cutting the lawn on a commercial farm tractor. There was a pond behind the house, and the family had picnics there. Robinson loved playing golf, and his own lawn was so big that he could practice at his own home for a change. And while the Robinsons' neighbors were all white families with young children of their own, there was no racism. Adults and children socialized without problems.

Jackie was glad to be home, satisfied to no longer be playing baseball. Once he quit the game, he rarely attended many baseball games. Not all his memories of baseball were happy ones, and he put that life behind him. Even so, Jackie was far from bitter. In thinking about how he felt about baseball once he was through with it, Jackie had this to say: "The way I figured it, I was even with baseball and baseball with me. The game had done much for me, and I had done much for it."

Robinson toured the country for the NAACP's Fight for Freedom Fund. The NAACP took on many court cases where black people were fighting for their rights, and it cost money. Though Robinson had often given inspirational speeches, he was not, at first, confident about his fundraising abilities. But everybody knew what he had done, how he had desegregated baseball and stood with dignity against so much abuse. Jackie's first speeches were barely five minutes long, but the crowds loved him so much that he was soon speaking for half an hour or longer—and raising a lot of money for the NAACP. In one city he made such a powerful speech that the entire audience rose up as one and began singing the Civil Rights anthem, "We Shall Overcome," adding "Jackie is our leader."

The high point of Jackie Robinson's speaking tour came in Oakland, California. He pointed out that there were 17,000,000 blacks in the country but only 350,000 NAACP members. In honest and straightforward words, Jackie inspired thousands. "The NAACP represents everything that a man should stand for," Jackie pointed out. "It stands for human dignity, brotherhood, and fair play." Soon, the NAACP membership increased dramatically.

In 1957, Jackie Robinson learned that he was suffering from diabetes, a disease that prevents the body from producing enough insulin. When Robinson saw a doctor, he was told that for a man his age—only thirty-eight—who had never drunk liquor or smoked, and was athletic, his body was in very poor shape. The pains Robinson had been suffering in his limbs had been telling him that something was wrong. It was very bad news, and Jackie was warned that diabetes could cause many problems, including heart disease and blindness. Robinson now injected himself with insulin on a daily basis, and he had to give up the sweets he loved so much. His weight fell by twenty pounds after his change in diet.

On March 3, 1957, Jackie Robinson began working at Chock Full o' Nuts as vice president of the company. He had much to learn in his new role, so Robinson threw himself into this challenge with great enthusiasm. He learned the locations of all 27 of the Chock Full o' Nuts restaurants, and he visited each of them to personally meet and talk with the employees. More than anything, Jackie wanted to help the workers and be a friend—not just a boss. When an employee got into legal trouble, Robinson went to court to support the employee's case. When immigrant employees wanted to bring family members into the country, Robinson interceded for them with the Immigration Service.

So, of course, Jackie hated having to fire an employee. Like his mother, it was Jackie's nature to help the underdog, not kick him. When Robinson had to sign dismissal papers, he said he felt like someone sending a prisoner to the electric chair. He said it was harder than anything he had been called on to do in his baseball career.

Race was also sometimes a problem for Robinson on his job. The black employees expected too much of him, and some white employees resented having a black boss. And because Bill Black, a white man, had hired so many black employees, some white people actually accused him of discrimination. At one point, the criticism from whites got so bad that Bill Black took out full-page ads in newspapers explaining that he couldn't care less about skin color as long as the employee did his or her job. But he also noted that blacks were unfairly discriminated against in employment—and he would continue doing his part to fight that discrimination.

Furthermore, "Mr. Black told me that if he were in my place, there wouldn't be enough he could do for the cause of freedom for black people," Jackie remembered. "He said he approved wholeheartedly of my participation [in the Civil Rights Movement]."

And it was a very important time for Jackie Robinson to be involved. Southern black people were still struggling for equality—it would be years before the federal Civil Rights Acts would be passed by Congress. Terrible things were still happening in the South to black people and the whites who supported them.

In 1955, Rosa Parks was tired from a long

day of work—and even more tired of racism. When she quietly refused to move to the back of a city bus in Montgomery, Alabama, she was dragged from the bus and arrested. "I felt that we had endured this too long," Parks explained.

In 1956, Dr. Martin Luther King, Jr.'s home in Montgomery, Alabama, was bombed, almost killing his baby daughter and wife. "We must use the weapon of love," Dr. King urged in a speech following the bombing. "We must have understanding for those who hate us."

Then, in 1957, nine black children tried to enter Central High School, which had previously been all white, in Little Rock, Arkansas. A screaming, threatening crowd of whites blocked their way. Several hundred National Guardsmen also helped keep the children out. Like Jackie Robinson, the nine children endured being spat on, verbally humiliated, and taunted. However, also like Jackie, the children would not be defeated—they returned again, only to be turned away again by a screaming crowd.

Finally, on September 24, President Eisenhower sent a thousand paratroopers to Little Rock, and he put the Arkansas National Guard under federal law. The white mob was stopped, and the nine children got inside Central High School for good. It was the first time since just after the Civil War that a president had used troops to protect the rights of blacks.

During this time President Eisenhower had asked for patience. Jackie believed in Dr. King's nonviolent approach and using the "weapon of love." But what happened in Little Rock reminded Robinson of the racist whites who tried to bar blacks from baseball. It badly tested Robinson's patience. And for black people all across the nation, patience had run out a long time ago. It was time for change—and Jackie Robinson intended to help bring about that change.

Chapter 9

Fighting for Equality

"We have waited almost one hundred years for [our] rights. . . . In my view, now is the time for Negroes to ask for all of the rights which are theirs." Jackie Robinson was speaking at an NAACP fundraising meeting in Chicago in 1957. Hundreds of attendees cheered Jackie's words—the time had come. The days of patiently waiting had ended. And while Jackie did not believe in violence, he believed even less in sitting idly by and simply hoping for change. So, in addition to working full time at Chock Full o' Nuts, Jackie worked tirelessly for that change.

Meanwhile, Rachel Robinson decided it was time for a change of her own. As a young woman, she had trained long and hard to become a nurse, and now she wanted to use her skills. She enrolled at New York University in downtown Manhattan to study for a master's degree in psychiatric nursing. Jackie Robinson was not completely happy about Rachel's decision, but he did not oppose it. "To be very honest," Jackie admitted, "if I had my way,

Rachel would not have a job . . . but I knew she was entitled to aspire to her own personal goals." And Rachel certainly achieved her goals. After finishing graduate school at 39, Rachel eventually became the director of nursing at Connecticut Medical Health Center and also an assistant professor in the School of Nursing at Yale University.

Though supporting the NAACP vigorously, sometimes Jackie Robinson wondered if it was too conservative in taking action against civil rights outrages. He often felt that the older ages of the board members (most of them over sixty) put them out of touch with the current troubles of young black people. For example, when Dr. Martin Luther King, Jr. was manhandled and arrested because of his leadership of civil rights protests, ten thousand people marched in protest in Washington, D.C. Dr. King's wife, Coretta Scott King, marched along with Jackie Robinson. And there were religious leaders from Protestant, Catholic and Jewish organizations present. But the NAACP did not participate. Robinson was bitterly disappointed with the NAACP and with the President of the United States. President Eisenhower, who had been so friendly to Jackie when they had met, had also refused to support the march.

And when Jackie Robinson joined another civil rights march that included 30,000 black and white civil rights activists singing "We Shall Overcome," President Eisenhower again refused to meet with them or support the march. Robinson had been very impressed by Eisenhower's personal warmth, but he was repeatedly bewildered by his public stance.

In January, 1959, Jackie Robinson turned forty. He now had a radio program, *The Jackie Robinson Show*, at WRCA in New York City. It was a half-hour interview show, with guests including mayors, governors, and sports figures. Jackie even interviewed Mrs. Eleanor Roosevelt, a strong supporter of civil rights. Robinson invited President Eisenhower and Vice President Nixon, but they did not appear.

When Robinson's two-year contract with Chock Full o' Nuts was running out, Bill Black renewed it for another five years. When people pointed out to Black that Robinson often said controversial things that might damage the company, Black responded defiantly. He said that if anybody wanted to boycott Chock Full o' Nuts over something Robinson said, he could recommend other good coffee places they could go to. Jackie's comments, in fact, helped the company. More and more frequently, people, black and white, were asking for "a can of that Jackie Robinson coffee" when they bought coffee at the grocery store.

In 1959, Jackie Robinson became a columnist for the *New York Post*. He wrote about many topics, including civil rights. In one of his most passionate columns, he denounced the all-too-frequent incidences of lynching blacks in the South. In Poplarville, Mississippi, a young black man was accused of raping a white woman. He was arrested and left in an unguarded jail. Soon a white mob arrived, dragged him out, beat him bloody, and murdered him. The man's body was discovered floating in the Pearl River. The FBI investigated the incident and found no federal law had been violated. But they turned all the results of their investigation over to the local law-enforcement officials, including the names of the men who had lynched the suspect. A local grand jury refused to indict anybody.

As the election of 1960 neared, Jackie Robinson mulled over the choices. At heart he was a liberal Republican, and he really liked the Republican candidate, Richard Nixon, as a man. They had enjoyed several warm conversations. Robinson believed Nixon supported civil rights legislation much more strongly than President Eisenhower did. "All great movements of reform start slowly and encounter bitter opposition," Nixon had once written. "But they soon gather an irresistible momentum and gain rapid acceptance. I . . . believe this will be the case in the battle for equal rights." Jackie was impressed. Eisenhower had never made such a supportive statement.

In addition, Robinson did not like Senator John F. Kennedy of Massachusetts, because he had recently hosted a meeting for some segregationist Southern politicians. Also, when Robinson met Kennedy, he noticed that Kennedy would not look him in the eye: "My mother had taught me to be wary of anyone with . . . shifty eyes," Robinson explained. And then

Kennedy chose Senator Lyndon Johnson of Texas as his vice-presidential running mate. Johnson was seen at the time as a man who favored segregation. So that made up Jackie Robinson's mind. He would support his old friend Richard Nixon for president. Even so, on Election Day, when John F. Kennedy became the next president, Jackie Robinson wished him well.

With the election over, Robinson could spend more of his free time with his family again. Jackie Jr. was now 14, Sharon was 10, and David was 8. Robinson was a sweet and loving father. He took David on fishing trips and to the golf course, where the boy was his dad's caddy. Robinson took Sharon on exciting trips into New York City, where they both shopped for clothes for Sharon and her mother. Jackie Robinson's relationship with his oldest son, Jackie Jr., was more of a problem. Robinson wanted the best for the boy who carried his name, and often he would gently urge him to study more and get better grades.

Jackie Robinson had broken into major league baseball when Jackie Jr. was just a baby. As a toddler, Jackie Jr. was a beautiful child with large dark eyes. When he was at the ballpark, fans would throng around him and make a fuss over him. He was Jackie Robinson's cute little namesake, and he became a celebrity too. People looked upon Jackie Jr. as an adorable mascot and gave him gifts because they loved his father. The small boy could not understand all this. His younger brother and sister did not experience anything similar, so they grew up in a more normal way.

Jackie Jr.'s brother and sister were independent spirits. But Jackie Jr. was a fearful child, often hanging back and unwilling to try new experiences. When it came time to learn how to swim, he hesitated. His sister, four years younger, jumped right in with a splash. But Jackie Jr. remained timidly standing on the diving board. While Sharon and David rode horses, Jackie Jr. would not go near a horse. And when it came to sports, Jackie Jr. was particularly shy. "At first," Robinson sadly remembered, "he enjoyed playing and was good at [baseball]. But he was exposed to cruel experiences, not so much by the youngsters as the parents, who made loud vocal comparisons between the way Jackie played and the way I played."

In high school, Jackie Jr.'s grades began sinking more and more. In time, he no longer seemed to care about anything, and Robinson felt a gap widening between himself and his oldest son: "I couldn't get through to him and he couldn't get through to me." Jackie Jr.'s worried parents took him to a psychiatrist, who suggested he should attend a private school for children having trouble adjusting. So Jackie Jr. was enrolled in Stockbridge School in Massachusetts. Rachel and Jackie Robinson hoped the new school would help their son with whatever problems he was having.

In 1961, John F. Kennedy appointed his brother

Robert Kennedy to the position of Attorney General of the United States. Jackie Robinson grew to like and admire Robert Kennedy for his passionate commitment to civil rights. Whenever there was an abuse of a black person in the South, Robert Kennedy swung into action.

In 1962, his first year of eligibility, Jackie Robinson was elected to the Baseball Hall of Fame. Robinson was so excited that he called Branch Rickey and his mother, Mallie, when he heard the good news. He became the first black American so honored, and Jackie was obviously pleased. However, when asked if he was happy with all the progress that had been made with integrating baseball, Jackie had to be honest. "I'll be more pleased," Jackie answered strongly, "the day I can look over at third base and see a black man as manager." Many people involved in professional baseball were angry to hear Robinson say this—the truth was hard to hear—but Robinson insisted on speaking it.

In the midst of all the wonderful publicity that followed the Hall of Fame induction, an ugly distraction arose. A neighborhood restaurant in New York, Lloyd's Steakhouse, was on West 125th Street. It was owned by a black man, Lloyd von Blaine, and it did a very good business. Suddenly a new steakhouse was moving into the area—a Sol Singer Steakhouse—which promised to sell steaks at a much cheaper price than Lloyd von Blaine was charging. Singer was white and Jewish. The black Lloyd's steakhouse feared ruin from this new, less expensive competition.

Black activists threatened to drive Singer out. They used anti-Semitic slogans. The whole situation seemed about to explode into a vicious black versus Jewish battle. Nearly all of the black leaders remained silent about the conflict, even if they disagreed with the blacks who were doing the name-calling. But Jackie would not sit by silently. In an angry article about the conflict, Jackie wrote: "Anti-Semitism is as rotten as anti-Negroism. It's a shame that, so far, none of the Negroes of Harlem have had the guts to say so . . ." This led to a hate campaign against Robinson for not siding with his own people. Carrying signs that read "Old Black Joe—Jackie Must Go!" and "His Mouth Is Too Big!" black activists picketed Chock Full o' Nuts and labeled Robinson a traitor.

Finally, Roy Wilkins of the NAACP came to Robinson's defense and also denounced the anti-Jewish campaign. In a telegram, Wilkins compared the threats and name-calling tactics of the black activists to the methods of the Ku Klux Klan. Then, a dynamic black pastor in Brooklyn asked all four hundred members of his church to patronize the Chock Full o' Nuts coffee shop in a show of support for Jackie Robinson's courageous stand against any and all forms of bigotry. This ended the bitter conflict, and Robinson was vindicated.

In late 1962, Jackie Robinson faced surgery to repair torn cartilage found in his left knee. He had a successful operation, but he had to wear an ankle-to-thigh cast. Suddenly grave complications developed. A vicious staphylococcal bacterial infection had attacked his knee. Jackie was in terrible pain as blood poisoning spread throughout his body. Robinson's diabetes went wild as a result of the blood disorder. The forty-four-year-old Robinson was near death, fading in and out of consciousness. To save his life, he was given penicillin and insulin injections. When Rachel Robinson came to his bedside, Jackie Robinson did not recognize her.

Slowly, Robinson recovered. Cards and flowers flooded the hospital. Eighty-two-year-old Branch Rickey was among the many visitors. Prayers and good wishes came from every corner of the country and around the world.

When Jackie Robinson finally was well enough to go home, he was greeted by bad news. Jackie Jr. had failed at Stockbridge School, and he was being sent home. Even though Jackie Jr. had not done well at Stockbridge, he seemed at peace at the local school, and his parents hoped the worst was over for their sixteen-year-old son.

Then, one day, Jackie Jr. simply vanished. No one seemed to have any idea as to why Jackie Jr. had left or where he had gone. Robinson, still weak from his illness, was now frantic with worry. Not knowing what else to do, he searched through his son's room, looking for any clues. "We didn't believe in rummaging through [our children's] things without their permission. But when Jackie disappeared, I felt justified," Robinson later wrote. Robinson didn't find any clues, but he did find something he would never forget. Folded carefully inside an old wallet of Jackie Jr.'s was a picture of Robinson. "It meant that Jackie Jr. had cared a lot more for his old man than his old man had guessed," Robinson said. "I broke down and cried in the terrible way a man cries when he's someone who never cries."

Finally a call came from Jackie Jr. He and a friend from school had caught a bus for California, hoping to get jobs picking fruit. Jackie explained that he wasn't "running away"—he just wanted to prove that he could make it on his own for once. But he had proved nothing. Jackie Jr. and his friend had been unable to find jobs, and now they were broke. Robinson sent his son money to return home on the same bus.

Aged and gray far beyond his years from illness and worry, Robinson slowly resumed his work and civil rights schedule. More and more, he began supporting the work of Martin Luther King, Jr., who was leading the fight to desegregate the South. One of King's battles involved the brutal Birmingham Police Chief Eugene "Bull" Connor, a bigot and a Klan member. When 2,000 peaceful black demonstrators marched in downtown Birmingham with King, Connor repaid their nonviolence with violence. He ordered his police to attack. Robinson watched the evening news, horrified by film of black protesters, mostly young people and teens, being attacked by police dogs and high-pressure fire hoses. The pressure of the hoses was strong enough to rip bark off trees—still, Connor ordered his men to use those hoses on defenseless women and children. In the end, Connor ordered 1,300 black children to be thrown in jail.

Robinson had seen enough. He went to Birmingham to join the protests, saying, "I don't like to be bitten by dogs . . . I don't like to go to jail . . . But we've got to show Martin Luther King that we are behind him." As he walked with the marchers in Birmingham, the sight of the silver-haired Hall-of-Famer leaning heavily on his cane touched many hearts.

In August 1963, 250,000 people, black and white, marched in support of civil rights in Washington, D.C. It was at this gathering that Dr. Martin Luther King delivered his famous "I Have a Dream" speech, asking for peace, nonviolence, and understanding. But only weeks after this speech, it seemed as if society was being ripped apart in America. The civil rights struggle turned deadly. In September of '63, the Sixteenth Street Baptist Church in Birmingham, Alabama, was bombed, killing four little girls attending Sunday school. Then, only two months later, President John F. Kennedy was assassinated. Jackie Robinson had not liked Kennedy at first, but he had come to admire his courage in doing more for civil rights than any American president before him. "When the tragic news [of the assassination] first hit," Robinson wrote in the *Amsterdam News*,

"I gasped with disbelief that here in America in 1963, a president could be murdered simply because he was a man of courageous conviction."

In February 1964, Jackie Robinson left Chock Full o' Nuts by mutual agreement. Robinson began to work for New York governor Nelson Rockefeller, a liberal Republican. Rockefeller was going to make a run for the presidency. Robinson did as much as he could for Rockefeller, but diabetes was taking its toll. Robinson's eyesight was failing, and his legs felt wobbly. Even his heart was now being affected by the ravages of the disease.

Robinson was only 45, and he still needed to be earning a salary. After leaving Chock Full o' Nuts, he was beginning to think about starting his own business again. He looked into banking, public relations, insurance, real estate, and the media. But he put his search on hold in his effort to help Nelson Rockefeller gain the Republican nomination for president. The biggest threat to Rockefeller's getting the nomination was the ultra-conservative Arizona senator, Barry Goldwater.

Robinson believed Goldwater posed a real and present danger to the advance of civil rights in America. Goldwater believed in states' rights over federal rights. All the progress blacks had made in ending segregation in schools, transportation, and other places had come through federal laws. The Southern states always resisted anti-segregation laws, so the idea of being in charge of making their own decisions about segregation was appealing to these states.

At the Republican convention, Jackie Robinson sat with the few black delegates—most blacks were Democrats. When Nelson Rockefeller rose to speak, he was drowned out by boos and shouts. It reminded Jackie of his reception in some ballparks during his early career in baseball. The convention was dominated by Goldwater supporters, and they did not want to hear anyone else. Goldwater was nominated Republican candidate for president. But in the election, President Lyndon Johnson, who had taken office when President Kennedy was assassinated, won by a landslide.

A worried Jackie Robinson saw a darkening racial future. He feared white backlash from some of the gains blacks had made. At the same time, black extremists, like Malcolm X, were beginning to preach violence as a way to deal with that backlash. Jackie often found it difficult to be as patient as Dr. Martin Luther King, but he disagreed strongly with Malcolm X. The journey to being "free at last" had different roads, but the destination, Jackie knew, was the same: "There's not an American in this country free," Jackie once wrote, "until every one of us is free."

Chapter 10

Jackie Robinson Steals Home

Jackie Robinson was never one to mince words. "Black people were coming to the point where they [were] crying out in support of Black Power," he wrote in the mid-sixties, "but it was pathetic to realize how little we knew of money." In addition, Jackie was irritated by how black people were repeatedly denied loans. But at the same time, blacks had no choice but to deposit their savings in the same banks that discriminated against them. As always, Jackie didn't wait around for a change—he made one.

In 1964, Jackie Robinson developed a bank in Harlem—Freedom National Bank—which would be owned by blacks to serve the community. He asked the people of Harlem to support this bank since, after all, it would be for their benefit. The bank opened on December 18, 1964. Congratulations came in from around the country. Robinson was excited and encouraged. He hoped this would be the first of many such banks that would help black people get a bigger piece of the economic pie.

Robinson was also encouraged by how President Lyndon Johnson was moving forward on the 1964 Civil Rights Act. President Johnson vowed to get it passed to honor the memory of the slain President Kennedy, who had been working for it when he died. The 1964 Civil Rights Act was passed, and then the 1965 Voting Rights Act was also passed to make sure all Americans, white and black, had the chance to vote.

But in the midst of all this good news, Jackie Robinson, Jr. was beginning to worry his parents again. Not long after running away to California, Jackie Jr. announced that he was going to join the Army. He was still obsessed with proving his own identity—not just being the "junior" version of his father. In addition, he thought the Army would be a great learning experience. "He was 17," Robinson recalled, "and he believed all the stories he heard about the opportunity the Army gave to travel— Jackie got to travel all right."

In June 1965, Jackie Robinson Jr. was sent to the jungles of Southeast Asia. The United States was involved in a war against the Communists in Vietnam which had been going on already for several years. But it was growing bigger and deadlier all the time as more American troops were sent in.

At one point, Jackie Jr. and his platoon were ambushed by enemy soldiers, and the soldiers on each side of Jackie Jr., two of his closest buddies, fell. The first friend died instantly, but the second friend cried out for help. Though wounded himself, Jackie Jr. dragged his wounded friend from the line of fire. But before Jackie Jr. could reach the medics, his friend died in his arms. Jackie Robinson, Jr. spent a week in the army hospital. Although he humbly downplayed his heroism, Jackie Jr. received the Purple Heart for suffering battle wounds in action.

In the midst of this difficult time, Robinson suffered another blow. In December 1965, Branch Rickey died, leaving Robinson deeply saddened. Rickey not only had given Robinson the chance to break down the color barrier for black players in the major leagues, but he had always remained loyal to Robinson. As Robinson left the funeral, reporters crowded around him, crassly asking how he felt about Rickey's death. "He filled a void for me," Jackie responded quietly. "I feel almost as if I had lost my own father. Mr. Rickey treated me like a son."

In June, 1966, Jackie Robinson, Jr. came home from Vietnam. His parents had hoped the military experience would be good for their son, but it did not turn out that way. Jackie Jr. had dramatically changed for the worse. The horror of the Vietnam War had drained away his good nature, as it had done to many young soldiers returning home. A close friend of Jackie Jr.'s remembered comments he had made not long after he returned home: "You talk to a guy in the morning, and you're putting him in a body bag in the afternoon. . . . No one really understands. Everyone tells me I'll get over it. But, man, I have nightmares every night."

Though he always had problems in school, Jackie Jr. had always been a sweet person. Now, that sweetness was gone. The once amiable youngster was now a strange and frightened man. On a trip to Montreal, he walked very close to the buildings lining the sidewalk, almost hugging them. He was reliving Vietnam, where he was always expecting a burst of gunfire, and the only safety lay in remaining close to walls. Robinson watched his son helplessly, not knowing how to reach him. And as Jackie Jr. drifted further and further away, he was becoming entangled in a secret nightmare that his parents knew nothing about.

In 1966, Robinson was appointed special assistant to Governor Nelson Rockefeller in charge of community affairs. The job paid $25,000—a salary that Robinson greatly welcomed with two children approaching college and the expensive home in Connecticut to keep up. At the same time, Rachel continued enjoying great success with her nursing and teaching. And though Jackie Jr. remained distant, he assured his parents that he was fine. Things seemed to be looking up for the Robinsons.

But then, on March 4, 1968, Jackie and Rachel became aware of their oldest son's secret nightmare—he was addicted to heroin. Jackie Robinson, Jr. was arrested and charged with possession of marijuana and heroin as well as having a .22 caliber revolver. Narcotics officers had interrupted a drug deal in downtown Stamford, and shots were fired. Jackie Jr. fled the scene but was later captured by the police and jailed. Prior to this, the young man had been found with drug paraphernalia, but he had gotten off by insisting it belonged to a friend. Jackie and Rachel had always believed their son when he told them he didn't do drugs. Jackie Jr. admitted to smoking a little pot now and then, but insisted it was the only drug he had tried. "He gave us the familiar argument that marijuana is harmless," Jackie later wrote, "that it only leads weak-minded people into the hard stuff. . . . He was convincing." And, unfortunately, Jackie and Rachel had been convinced.

Robinson's first gut reaction to the news was to leave his son in jail—he was that angry. But in his heart, he knew that Jackie Jr. needed his parents more than ever. They posted the $5,000 bail, and Rachel Robinson arranged for her son to be sent to Yale-New Haven Hospital, where she worked. He would be evaluated there to see what kind of drug habit he had. As the Robinsons left the jail, reporters crowded around, peppering them with questions. Jackie Robinson replied to the questions in a sorrowful whisper. Rachel and Sharon Robinson were crying, but Jackie Robinson, bent over now with graying hair, was dry-eyed and stoic.

On April 7, Jackie Robinson, Jr. was given

the choice of going to jail or enrolling in a strict rehabilitation program. Because he was a first offender and a Vietnam veteran, he was offered a break. He chose rehab. And the truth slowly began to unfold. Two court-appointed doctors said he had been addicted to heroin for about six months. As the pressures of the Vietnam War increased, many of the young Americans in combat used marijuana. When they returned home, they were hooked, and Jackie Jr. was one of the victims. First he got high on marijuana, pills and cough syrup. Once he was home in New York, his drug habit grew to include more serious substances. He started using cocaine, LSD and amphetamines. And one night, even though he was afraid to stick a needle into his own arm, he tried heroin. In a frightening blur, Jackie Jr. quickly became hooked. Finally, he began stealing: "I was into every type of crime that you could get into, in order to support my drug habit," Jackie Jr. admitted.

The Robinsons recalled a letter they had received from their son when he was in Vietnam. The American soldiers had killed a Communist (Viet Cong) sniper who was picking off Americans. They tied his dead body to the front of their jeep, just like hunters who had shot a deer. They drove through Vietnamese villages warning the people that if they joined the Communist side, this might happen to them too. The horror of that incident imprinted itself on Jackie Robinson, Jr.'s mind, and he kept seeing it replayed. He also told his parents about six of his buddies being killed in one week. Jackie Jr. called Vietnam "the most miserable place in the world," and he did not understand what the United States was doing there.

The brutality and ugliness of war was not the only trauma in young Robinson's life. A second shock, for him, was confronting racism for the first time in his life. He had grown up in friendly Stamford, Connecticut, where the majority of whites and the Robinsons and their friends got along like one big happy family. Jackie Robinson himself had experience with racial prejudice as a boy, and so he was prepared. However, Jackie Robinson, Jr. was wholly unprepared for the racial taunting he found in the Army.

On the evening of April 4th, 1968, Dr. Martin Luther King, Jr. stood on the balcony of the Lorraine Motel in Memphis, Tennessee. Dr. King had gone to Memphis to help black sanitation workers, who were striking for better treatment in the workplace. It had been a long and sometimes difficult day, but now Dr. King was out on the balcony, smiling and chatting with friends. Suddenly, a single shot blasted through the evening calm. Within seconds, the man who had worked tirelessly for equality for more than a decade, who had patiently preached a nonviolent approach, lay dead on the balcony.

All over America, in major cities, angry blacks surged into the streets. There was widespread rioting and looting. Jackie Robinson had worked with Dr. King, walked with him during demonstrations, and he admired him greatly. He was deeply saddened at the loss of this great black man. Robinson was also sickened by the rioting that followed, knowing that it was exactly the sort of thing that Dr. King would not have wanted: violence as a response to violence.

1968 was a devastating year for all America. The loss of American lives in Vietnam was skyrocketing. Dr. King had been assassinated, and the entire country had lost a great man. But Jackie Robinson also endured personal loss. Jackie felt that in a very real way he had lost his son to drugs, though his faith kept him believing that his son would return to him one day. Then, on May 21, 1968, Jackie's mother Mallie died. It took all the courage Robinson could muster to look into the face of the mother who had loved him so long and so well and to realize he would not see her again on this Earth. What consoled him the most was the look of total peace on her gentle face.

And then, only a month after Mallie's death, Jackie, and the entire nation, were stunned by another death. Jackie Robinson had developed great admiration for Robert Kennedy, the younger brother of John F. Kennedy. He was now a New York senator and candidate for president in the 1968 election, and he had done a great deal to advance the civil rights causes Robinson struggled for. Then, in June 1968, Robert Kennedy was shot and killed by an assassin in Los Angeles.

Jackie Robinson, Jr. was now a resident at Daytop Rehabilitation in Seymour, Connecticut, a well-regarded narcotics treatment center. Hard discipline was used to help the patients—no one was given sympathy or any breaks. The Daytop philosophy was that patients must prove that they need and want to recover. The staff consisted of reformed drug addicts who had once been patients themselves, and their own hard-won experience made them tough and smart in dealing with young people like Robinson. When Robinson raved and cried as he went through heroin withdrawals, the staff gave him no pity or comfort. It was an unusual approach back then, but it worked.

Once over his withdrawals, Jackie Jr. proved that he truly wanted the help of Daytop. Even so, the staff warned the Robinsons that Jackie Jr. would reach a breaking point and would call home, asking for someone to come and get him. "You must inform him that he cannot come home," Daytop advised the Robinsons. "You must tell him that you will have him picked up by the police if he tries . . . that you will have his bail revoked and let him go to jail." The Robinsons prayed that this moment would not arise, but eventually it did. "Can you imagine the anguish of being a parent and having to [tell that] to a son you love?" Jackie wrote years later. But the tough love worked—for a while.

Only a few weeks after Jackie Jr. had asked his parents to come and get him, he left without permission. He was later arrested in a Stamford hotel room. He had pointed a gun at the arresting officers and could have been killed if the officer had not used restraint. Jackie Jr. was given a suspended sentence of two to four years in prison and was allowed to return to Daytop for more help. Perhaps Jackie Jr. had finally hit rock bottom. But for whatever reason, once he returned to Daytop, he began to take his recovery seriously.

On January 31, 1969, Jackie Robinson turned fifty years old. A big birthday celebration with friends and family was held at the Robinsons' Connecticut home. Although Robinson's health continued to be a serious worry, he seemed in high spirits that day. There had been many good reports from Daytop on the progress of Jackie Jr., and there was reason to hope he was at last on track for completing the program and being released as a healthy, drug-free man. It was, quite possibly, this good news that revived a bit of the mischievous Jackie of the old days.

Back behind the big house was a pond that, as usual in January, was frozen solid. Suddenly, without even a hint of warning, Jackie jumped onto a sled and went sailing down the hill toward the pond. Everybody watched in disbelief and fright as the big man on the sled sailed out across the frozen pond. Jackie Robinson turned and erupted into a roar of deep, satisfied, gleeful laughter. For just a moment, on this cold night, Jackie Robinson was young again. The stocky, stooped, silver-haired man with the bad knees, the bad legs, the failing heart and eyesight was a boy once more.

In 1970, the Freedom National Bank was firmly established as the most successful black-controlled bank in the United States. The Jackie Robinson Construction Company was building homes, and things seemed to be on the upswing again. David Robinson, the youngest son, was doing well in school and would be going to Stanford University in California in the fall. Sharon Robinson was married to a man her parents liked, and she was studying to be a nurse like her mother.

Jackie Robinson, Jr. had come home for Christmas, but on his own he realized he needed more time at Daytop, so he returned there. The fact that Jackie Jr. had made this decision for himself was immeasurably encouraging to Jackie and Rachel. They were so indebted to the work of Daytop that they decided to host a large picnic for members of Daytop on the grounds of their home. Jackie Jr. seemed happier than anyone had seen him in a long time, and on that day something happened that meant the world to Jackie Robinson. When his son had left for the army, he had hugged his mother in saying goodbye, but when his father had tried to hug him, he pushed him away and stiffly shook his hand instead. That left the elder Robinson deeply hurt. But now, at the picnic, when the young man again hugged his mother, and his father offered his hand for a handshake, Jackie Jr. pushed the hand aside and instead gave his father a bear hug. "That single moment paid for every bit of sacrifice, every bit of anguish, I had undergone," Jackie recalled. "I had my son back."

Jackie Robinson was now always weary, and his feet and legs ached. Tests showed that the diabetes was worsening rapidly. Jackie started to get severe wheezing and coughing spells at night along with shortness of breath. Only by kneeling by the side of his bed and bending over could he get his breath back. Ruptured blood vessels in his eyes had seriously damaged his vision. The once bright-eyed athlete who stole bases and hit home runs was slowly going blind. Rachel Robinson took a leave of absence from her job at Yale to help care for her husband. There was deep sorrow and worry in Rachel Robinson's heart. She was so sad that she went into therapy to help her cope with what seemed to be coming—the loss of her beloved husband.

Still, Jackie Robinson pushed on, being as cheerful as he could be and fulfilling his duties. The kind of raw courage he displayed on the baseball field when he stood against so many taunts and attacks still motivated him now. He would not retire to his bed and accept that he was sick and useless. He still had work to do. In addition, his son was finally free from drug addiction. Jackie Jr. had beaten his nightmare, and he was quickly hired as a leader at Daytop. Now he would do for others what they had done for him. Although Robinson's sight was dimming, his son's success was like a brilliant light shining in his life. But that light shone only briefly before a dark night seemed to swallow it up.

On June 17, the doorbell roused Jackie Robinson in the middle of the night. He arrived at the door at the same time as his daughter. A police officer with a grim look on his face stood there. His message was devastating. There had been a terrible auto accident. Jackie Robinson Jr. was driving his small car back from a Daytop fundraising meeting in New York City when he lost control. The car went into a deadly spin, hitting a wall. Jackie Jr. suffered a broken neck. He was taken from the crushed vehicle and pronounced dead.

Rachel Robinson was at a conference in Massachusetts, and Jackie knew that he had to tell her the horrible news in person and that he must get to her before she heard it on the radio or saw it on the news. Without a moment to spare, Jackie and his daughter, Sharon, jumped in the car and drove up to Massachusetts, arriving at Rachel's hotel just as the sun was rising. When Rachel saw her daughter and husband's faces, she knew something terrible had happened. Upon hearing the news, Rachel collapsed, overcome by grief.

On June 21, fifteen hundred people attended Jackie Robinson, Jr.'s funeral at Antioch Baptist

Church in Brooklyn. Cars jammed the streets for blocks, and mourners overflowed down the steps of the church and into the streets. Jackie recalled that "the minister spoke of Jackie Jr. as a hero—in Vietnam and in the larger war he had to fight when he came back home." Covered in flowers, the bronze casket was taken to Cypress Hills Cemetery. There, the firstborn child of Jackie and Rachel Robinson was laid to rest.

Jackie Robinson remained strong after his son's death. His steadfast faith in God and his certain belief in an afterlife, where he would be reunited with his beloved son, supported him. But Rachel Robinson was not so strong. For a while her husband thought he had lost her too. She withdrew into a dark place. She worried that she had somehow failed her son, and that had led to his death. She could not understand why he was taken when he had done so well at Daytop and now was rebuilding his life. Finally, through the love of her husband and her children, Rachel Robinson was able to overcome her grief and live again.

As his father's sight failed, David Robinson drove him around. Jackie continued to go to the offices of his business, and he was available for speeches. At Christmas, 1971, the whole family took a vacation to Jamaica. On his return, Jackie Robinson delivered more speeches, and in the spring of 1972, he delivered the commencement address at Bethune-Cookman College in Daytona

Beach, Florida. He was fifty-two years old, but he walked like a man in his eighties or older.

Jackie Robinson made his last public appearance before the second game of the World Series on October 14, 1972 in Cincinnati. Robinson spoke with his usual passion, but it was obvious to everyone at the game that he was in extremely poor health. After Jackie threw out the first ball at Riverfront Stadium, and while he was being helped back to his seat, a young man came up to him. The man held out a baseball for Jackie to autograph, but Jackie shook his head, explaining that his eyesight was so bad that he'd likely write on top of the other autographs on the ball, ruining it. The young man put his hand on Jackie's shoulder and quietly said, "There are no other names, Mr. Robinson. The only one I want is yours."

On October 24, 1972, Jackie Robinson had a scheduled speaking engagement in Washington to talk about the dangers of drug abuse. But at 6:26 in the morning, Rachel Robinson called for am ambulance—Jackie was gripping his chest and struggling for air. Two police officers arrived to administer oxygen. The ambulance came and picked up Jackie Robinson, heading for Stamford Hospital. But Jackie died before they could reach the hospital. His great heart had finally stopped beating.

Tributes to Jackie poured in from all over the country. Instead of flowers, well-wishers were asked to make a donation to Daytop. Then, on October 29, the funeral was held at Riverside Church. Reverend Jesse Jackson delivered the eulogy. In his ringing voice, he cried out, "Jackie Robinson has stolen home!" Six former athletes carried the silver-blue and red-rose-draped casket. One of them was Bill Russell, a star basketball player with the Boston Celtics. All the others were old Brooklyn Dodgers who had played with Robinson, among them Pee Wee Reese. The funeral procession stretched for many city blocks, arriving at Cypress Hills Cemetery, where Jackie Robinson was buried next to his son.

After Jackie Robinson's death, the Robinsons honored his memory in special ways. Rachel Robinson set up the Jackie Robinson Development Corporation, which built homes for the poor and middle-class people. She also established the Jackie Robinson Foundation, which gives scholarships and leadership training to youth. Sharon, the Robinsons' daughter, is vice president of the Jackie Robinson Foundation; and David, the youngest son, is on the Board of Directors.

Jackie Robinson once said, "A life is not important except in the impact it has on other lives." Jackie's life had an immeasurable impact that touched, and continues to touch, many more lives than Jackie could probably have ever imagined. When Jackie first met Dr. Martin Luther King, Jr., Dr. King told him that his brave example of integrating baseball was the inspiration for much of the work that he, Dr. King, had done. While Jackie was surely flattered by King's words, it was, perhaps, the inspiration Jackie gave to the young, the unknown, and the hopeful that meant the most to him.

The day of Jackie Jr.'s funeral, the Robinsons walked sadly out of the church when the service was over. Tears still blurring his fading eyes, Jackie looked over to the funeral car. There seemed to be a group of children gathered near it, but Jackie could not quite make out what they were doing. As he got closer, the young black boys all grouped together and smiled respectfully—every one of them was wearing a baseball uniform.

In the midst of one of his darkest days, it was a bright moment Jackie would never forget. "For me," Jackie wrote later, "they signified that none of the suffering had been in vain. They were the bright hope of tomorrow. They were the age Jackie Jr. had been when I dreamed that what I was doing in baseball might make things easier for the kids of the following generations." At that moment, Robinson was shown, in the simplest of ways, that his life had been important indeed.

Upon Jackie's death, the most famous sports announcer of the time, Howard Cosell, said of Jackie, "He was incomparable." Understanding this, the game of baseball quickly retired his number. No player ever again would wear the number 42. For as long as baseball endures, it will remain enshrined in the Baseball Hall of Fame.

But on Sunday, April 15, 2007, on the 60th anniversary of Jackie Robinson's breaking the color barrier in major league baseball, every Los Angeles Dodger wore the number 42 on his back. So did every St. Louis Cardinal and Milwaukee Brewer, as well as at least one player on every other team that played that day. Ten big-league ballparks—it would have been all fifteen, but five games were postponed because of rain—held ceremonies remembering Jackie Robinson. The one in Los Angeles, however, was special.

In pre-game ceremonies, Rachel Robinson was honored. The Brookinaires Gospel Choir from the First African Methodist-Episcopal Church sang Jackie Robinson's favorite hymn, "Oh Happy Day." And then the game began.

The Dodgers stole five bases, their highest total in eight years. They collected 13 hits, and they beat the San Diego Padres. Jackie's fighting spirit was right there with them.

The great Hank Aaron said of Jackie Robinson and his courageous pioneering feat, "I don't know how he withstood the things he did without lashing back." Aaron concluded, "Somehow though, Jackie had the strength to suppress his instincts, to sacrifice his pride for his people. It was an incredible act of selflessness that brought the races closer together than ever before and shaped the dreams of an entire generation."

Jackie Robinson was one of the few athletes in American history to rise above the level of sports hero and become something far more—a human hero. He was not just one of the greatest second basemen of all time. Through his strength, determination, and quiet suffering, this brave man earned a permanent spot in American history. He was the first to rip down the shameful wall of racial segregation in our country's sports. For black people everywhere, and for all people dedicated to justice and human decency, he was and is a shining light. He is a true citizen of the world, and the heroic light he provides will burn forever.